LONDON B

KEN GLAZIER

Capital Transport

INTRODUCTION

This is one of a series of handbooks, each of which contains a complete list of all buses and coaches owned by London Transport during a period of four or five years, together with a brief description and history of each type covered. Vehicles which either joined or left the fleet during the period under review are listed with an additional column showing the dates on which they were formally taken into or removed from stock. These refer to the dates on which ownership changed and, in the case of buses taken out of stock, do not necessarily coincide with the day on which a vehicle left London Transport's hands physically. Vehicles sold for scrap were often dispatched to the breaker's yard before the paperwork was completed and some vehicles were stored by London Transport for a time after being sold to other operators. Where a body was scrapped before the chassis, the date on which the chassis was scrapped is deemed to be the date the complete vehicle was written off.

For the years after 1942 dates 'into stock' for all but experimental buses refer to the day on which the completed vehicle was received from the body builder. The chassis will have been owned for some time before this, however, as the normal procedure was for chassis to be delivered formally to London Transport, either physically or as a book transaction, before being sent for bodying.

This volume covers the period from 1st January 1940 to 31st December 1945, during most of which the United Kingdom was at war with Germany and Japan. Vehicle production for civilian use was severely limited and the government exercised strict control over the allocation of the few buses built. Although the original order for 150 RTs was completed, increasing shortages of materials slowed down their delivery which was not completed until 1942. These, with the last few CRs, were the only buses built to London Transport's own specification which entered service between 1940 and 1945. 'Unfrozen' chassis allocated to London Transport provided small additions to the STL and STD classes and created a new class B before the delivery of fully austerity buses in the G, D and B classes got under way from 1942 onwards. London Transport's vehicle replacement programme came to a virtual standstill and, once the vehicles already in store awaiting disposal had gone, most buses taken out of stock during this period were victims of bombing. A substantial shift to double-deck operation nevertheless rendered a large number of single-deckers surplus to requirements and many Cs and petrol-engined Ts were sent to the continent where they were used by the Allied Control Commission in their relief activities

These books would not have been possible without the generous help of Dr Andrew Gilks, from whose private collection the bulk of the information concerning dates has been derived. Others who have given assistance include Reg Westgate who has helped to fill the various gaps, and Les Stitson who has worked hard on checking the accuracy of the basic data. Special thanks are due to Mrs Thornton Jones for making available to the author her late husband's considerable collection of photographs, from which a number have been chosen for this volume. Thanks are also due to Brian Bunker, John Gent, Malcolm Papes and Dave Ruddom for allowing me to raid their photographic collections for illustrations and to the photographers, who are acknowledged separately in the body of the book, for permitting the use of their work.

First published 1999
ISBN 185414 216 X
© Capital Transport Publishing, Harrow Weald, Middlesex

CONTENTS

Title page
An Inter-Station bus service linking Paddington, Victoria, Waterloo, Euston and Kings Cross main line termini between 6.30pm and midnight daily was restored on 20th December 1943. One of four Cubs allocated at this time was C 112, seen at Waterloo station on 31st December. *Southern Railway*

Front cover
Twenty lowbridge bodies were built for STL chassis in 1942 and 1943 of the design shown on STL 2250 in full wartime apparel. *A painting by Barry Pearce*

Three former TDs returned to London service in October 1940 as part of the fleet of 'provincial' buses sent on loan to cover alleged vehicle shortages following the blitz. TD 160, formerly a Country Bus vehicle, was a Short Brothers bodied TD1 dating from 1930, originally owned by Maidstone & District Motor Services. Now owned by Youngs Bus Service of Paisley, it is seen at East Ham 'White Horse' terminus, familiar territory for its Central Bus counterparts when they were allocated to Upton Park garage. The enclosed staircase forty-eight seat body was a close imitation of the standard Leyland model of the time. D.W.K. Jones

TD

None of the vehicles in the TD class was purchased new by London Transport. The entire class of 195 vehicles came to the Board from other operators, mostly by compulsory acquisition under the terms of the London Passenger Transport Act of 1933. Included in the total were three single-deck buses and eighteen coaches. There were examples of both TD1 and TD2 type chassis, of petrol and oil engines, and six makes of body of various designs and capacities. By the beginning of 1940 all had been withdrawn from service but there were still 113 in stock awaiting disposal, which took place during 1940. Ironically, three of the sold buses came back to London in October 1940 as part of the fleet of 'provincial' vehicles which were sent in answer to an appeal for help following losses during the blitz, which London Transport claimed had left them short of buses.

Chassis:	Leyland Titan TD1 (TD 2, 3, 5–10, 17–20, 22, 24, 25, 28, 32, 34, 38, 43, 45–47, 50, 52–55, 57, 59, 61, 63, 65, 66, 69, 79–82, 89, 91, 94, 96, 103–107, 122, 126–129, 133–151, 154–166, 170, 171, 173, 192–195); Leyland Titan TD1spl (TD 112–121); Leyland Titan TD2 (TD 11, 12, 27, 29, 37, 98, 108, 123–125, 130)
Engine:	Leyland 6-cylinder 6.8 litre ohc 98 bhp petrol (TD1s); Leyland 6-cylinder 7.6 litre ohc 98 bhp petrol (TD2s); Leyland 6-cylinder 8.1 direct injection 87 bhp oil (TD 94, 96, 98, 105, 121)
Transmission:	Leyland 4-speed crash
Bodywork:	Birch (TD 37, 79–82); Dodson (TD 2, 3, 5–12, 17–20, 22, 24, 25, 27–29, 32, 34, 38, 43, 45–47, 50, 52–55, 57, 65, 89, 91, 94, 96, 98, 103–108, 112–130, 170, 171); Duple (TD 59, 61, 63, 66, 69); Leyland (TD 173, 194, 195); Short Bros (TD 133–151, 154–166); Weymann (TD 192, 193)
Capacity:	H30/26RO (TD 8, 20, 27, 28, 32, 37, 43, 45, 79–82, 96, 98, 106–107, 112, 114–120); H30/26R (TD 124) H30/24RO (TD 52, 57, 113, 121); H30/24R (TD 154, 155, 165, 166); H28/26RO (TD 46, 89, 91, 94); H28/26R (TD 108); H28/26RO (TD 18, 19); H28/24RO (TD 3, 5–7, 9, 10, 22, 24, 25, 34, 38, 50, 53–55, 59, 61, 63, 65, 66, 69, 103–105, 122, 126–129); H27/26R (TD 11, 12, 29, 130); H27/24R (TD 133–142, 173, 192–195); H26/26R (TD 30, 123); H26/24RO (TD 143–145, 147–151); H26/24R (TD 170); H25/26R (TD 125); H24/24RO (TD 2, 17, 47, 146); H24/24R (TD 156–164, 171)
Built:	1928–1932

Number acquired: 195
Number in stock: 1.1.40: 113; Last vehicle out of stock: 6.6.40

TD		Date out of stock	TD		Date out of stock	TD		Date out of stock
2	GJ8489	12.2.40	69	GK896	26.4.40	137	KJ1914	13.4.40
3	GC3354	16.5.40	79	GN5880	5.4.40	138	KJ1915	25.5.40
5	GC7493	12.4.40	80	GN5881	3.4.40	139	KJ1919	12.4.40
6	GC1804	13.5.40	81	GO1525	6.4.40	140	KJ1920	29.4.40
7	MY2742	3.4.40	82	GO1526	18.4.40	141	KJ1934	9.4.40
8	HX2643	16.5.40	89	UW2309	6.6.40	142	KJ1935	18.4.40
9	UW6777	3.4.40	91	UW2311	24.4.40	143	KO7338	30.4.40
10	GN4832	3.4.40	94	GC3172	6.4.40	144	KO7340	24.4.40
11	GW550	18.3.40	96	GX2602	6.4.40	145	KO7343	19.4.40
12	GY2042	21.3.40	98	JJ1269	10.4.40	146	KP3055	9.4.40
17	GK608	16.4.40	103	GO1636	15.4.40	147	KP3056	6.6.40
18	GP168	23.4.40	104	VX4269	23.4.40	148	KP3057	24.4.40
19	GP2512	24.4.40	105	VX5859	10.4.40	149	KP3061	6.4.40
20	GW738	24.4.40	106	VX8831	10.4.40	150	KP3065	26.4.40
22	HV453	22.4.40	107	VX8835	17.5.40	151	KP3067	9.4.40
24	HV898	22.5.40	108	EV7308	12.4.40	154	KR1721	25.4.40
25	HV1188	22.4.40	112	GO1933	3.4.40	155	KR1722	3.4.40
27	HV2822	26.3.40	113	GO1932	24.4.40	156	KR1723	13.4.40
28	GP3379	3.4.40	114	GO1346	15.5.40	157	KR1724	6.4.40
29	EV5860	27.3.40	115	GO1930	24.4.40	158	KR1725	14.5.40
32	GO4367	5.4.40	116	GW2758	15.5.40	159	KR1726	16.4.40
34	HV190	17.5.40	117	GW2759	16.5.40	160	KR1727	20.4.40
37	GW1285	27.3.40	118	GW2760	10.4.40	161	KR1728	12.4.40
38	UV5764	24.4.40	119	GW2761	13.5.40	162	KR1730	15.4.40
43	GK8779	6.6.40	120	GW2762	3.4.40	163	KR1732	17.4.40
45	GK9834	17.5.40	121	GX1839	15.4.40	164	KR1734	26.4.40
46	GT1083	15.5.40	122	UW4198	3.4.40	165	KR6835	3.4.40
47	GJ3435	26.4.40	123	EV6510	21.3.40	166	KR8396	3.4.40
50	GK8925	24.4.40	124	EV6692	17.4.40	170	UR6729	6.4.40
52	MY1315	10.4.40	125	EV8335	21.3.40	171	UR6730	6.4.40
53	MY1140	16.4.40	126	VX4261	12.4.40	173	UR9240	17.4.40
54	HX2492	15.5.40	127	MY2643	3.4.40	192	KJ2577	14.5.40
55	GC6664	24.5.40	128	MY2917	3.4.40	193	KJ2578	16.5.40
57	VX5169	19.4.40	129	MY4043	6.6.40	194	KJ2579	6.4.40
59	GJ7537	30.4.40	130	MV1376	16.4.40	195	KJ2580	25.5.40
61	GH889	17.4.40	133	KJ1906	9.4.40			
63	GH890	22.5.40	134	KJ1910	17.5.40			
65	UV5906	6.6.40	135	KJ1911	15.4.40			
66	GK893	24.5.40	136	KJ1912	11.4.40			

The first forty-nine production Renowns and LT 1 had square cabs, as seen on the LT2 body of LT 35 at Old Town, Clapham Common. Changes made for operation in the blackout include mudguards and platform edging painted white, a route number stencil hung over the rear lower saloon window, where it could be illuminated from within, and masks fitted over the headlamps. These were of the improved type designed by London Transport which replaced the original version in the summer of 1940. Malcolm Papes

LT

The LT class was the first of three new models introduced by the LGOC in 1929 and became the company's standard bus for a time between 1930 and 1932. LT 1–150 were the last LGOC buses to be built with open staircases and the first to go into production from the outset with covered tops (codes LT1, 2 and 2/1). LT 1 seated fifty-four, the rest sixty. The next 350 were to the same basic design but with enclosed straight staircases and full width rear platforms which reduced their seating capacity to fifty-six (code LT3). These were followed by three hundred of an improved version with inward sloping upper deck sides and a destination indicator set into the cab roof (LT4, 5 and variants). The last 150 of these were given substantially improved indicators incorporating separate route number, intermediate point and destination displays at the front (LT5/1). The remaining 272 LTs, plus one prototype (known as 'Bluebirds'), were the first LGOC buses to have the upper deck extended over the driver's cab and established the basic design layout which was to endure for the next thirty years (LT6, 8 and variants). Their very upright design, combined with a curved staircase and half-width platform, allowed a seating capacity of sixty to be achieved. LT 1137 was an experimental Green Line coach with a fifty-seat forward-entrance body finished internally to coach standards of seating and trim. It was converted to bus use in 1935 but was withdrawn from passenger service in 1942.

The rear view of LT 35 shows the characteristic London design of open staircase and the pre-war arrangement of route number stencil above the registration plate on the bulkhead, which was abandoned when restricted indicator displays were introduced later in the war. It is standing alongside STL 2495, both buses displaying the white spot which was a wartime embellishment peculiar to London Transport's motor buses. Malcolm Papes collection

All but one had the short-wheelbase Renown 663 chassis and were twenty-seven feet long but LT 1137 was mounted on one of the long wheelbase 664 version originally intended for a single-decker but was only six inches longer than the buses because its rear overhang was shorter (coded 1/1LTL2). The LT class was used as a test bed for developing oil engines and preselective transmission which, together with the development of the body design, established the basis of the standard specification for the rest of the 1930s. Experiments with oil engines started in March 1931 when LT 191–199 were fitted with AEC Acro A155 engines but they were not successful and were later modified to the improved Ricardo A161 version. A further twenty-three were fitted with the A161 engine, including three transferred from STs (coded 4LT) and one, experimental 'Bluebird' LT 741, a Gardner 6LW (9LT). The last seventy-two LTs all had oil engines. Sixty-two (LT 1355–1416; 8LT, 7LT and 10LT) had the new AEC A165 8.8 litre Ricardo engine but the last ten were powered by Gardner 6LW engines whose greater length required a shortened body and caused the bonnet to extend forwards in a snout (9LT7). A total of seventy-four LTs was fitted with either Wilson or Daimler epicyclic gearboxes and fluid transmission, fifty-four petrol-engined (3LT and 6LT) and twenty oil (8LT).

In 1933 and 1934 all the petrol engined crash gearbox 'Bluebirds' (170 buses, recoded 11LT) and 168 of the 151–949 batch (recoded 12LT) were given new A165 oil engines and their petrol engines were fitted to new STL chassis. A similar exchange, involving

The LT2/1 bodies had the rounded cab which was standard on Chiswick bodies built in 1930 and 1931 but was otherwise similar to the LT2 and formed the basis of the LT3 closed staircase design. LT 140, photographed in Grosvenor Gardens, Victoria, had been fitted with the wartime restricted blind display which was to remain standard on the type until it was withdrawn. Another wartime change was the installation of a route number stencil in the window of the fifth bay. *Frank Willis*

twenty-four buses, was made with new LTC coaches in 1937. A further 550 LTs were fitted with 8.8 litre oil engines in 1939 and 1940 (1/12LT) but this time their petrol engines were scrapped, the new A180 engine being so economical that there was strong financial justification for the outlay. For this reason all the earlier A165 engines were converted to direct injection between 1940 and 1943. One other Renown, LT 21, was fitted with an oil engine, in 1935, but this was a 7.7 litre A171 engine (the type used in STLs). With the completion of the conversion programme in January 1940 the only remaining petrol-engined double-deck LTs were the 150 open staircase buses (allocated to Leyton, Loughton and Potters Bar garages) and the fifty-four fitted with preselective gearboxes, which were all at Plumstead. The oil-engined Renowns were concentrated at eighteen garages, fifteen of which had no other type of double-decker.

At the beginning of 1940 all but the four LGOC-built CC LTs were still in stock. Their sphere of operations had been widened during the autumn of 1939 following the heavy cuts in service which followed the declaration of war, Old Kent Road, Potters Bar and West Green being added to the garages to which they were allocated and the partial allocations at Norwood and Upton Park being topped up to a full complement.

Withdrawal of the oldest LTs should have started in 1940 but the embargo on new vehicle construction during the Second World War extended the lives of most of them by up to ten years. Twenty double-deck LTs were destroyed in a single incident when Elmers End garage was hit by a V1 flying bomb. Many more were damaged to a greater or lesser degree in bombing or machine-gunning incidents and a large number received spare bodies from the float to replace those which were beyond repair. Apart from the outright losses, all the AEC LTs were still in stock at the end of 1945, including all the petrol-engined and Bluebird-bodied examples.

The enclosed staircase LT3 bodywork was a direct descendant of the LT2/1 which it resembled in most respects. LT 636, photographed towards the end of the war, had been fitted with the final design of combination headlamp and mask, introduced in 1943. This can be recognised by the projecting half-moon shaped hood which was designed to throw the maximum amount of light onto the road ahead. W.J. Haynes

The upper deck of the LT5 bodies had an inward slope which improved their appearance compared with earlier designs although perhaps their most distinctive feature was the indicator box set in the cab roof, which earned them the nickname 'camel-back'. Before restricted displays were introduced, there was a 'via' board set in the centre panel above the cab, illuminated by a lamp which is still present but unused on Norwood's LT 858, seen alongside the ruins of Crystal Palace. W.J. Haynes

LT 851, at Southend Crescent Eltham, was one of 150 Renowns mounted with LT5/1 bodies, which differed from the LT5 in having separate route number, intermediate point and destination boxes. By the time of this photograph a restricted display had replaced the full arrangement for good. W.J. Haynes

The apotheosis of the double-deck Renown in London was the elegant 'Bluebird' of 1932, which had the upper deck brought forward over the cab for the first time. LT 1232 is on the stand at Gidea Park (Gallows Corner) where it betrays signs of wartime short-cuts in its painted radiator and other bright parts. W.J. Haynes

Improved route indicators were provided at the back of the LT5/1s and the LT6 family of bodies by the addition of an intermediate point display above the combined number and destination box of the earlier designs. The windows of Bluebird LT 1210 have been fitted out with the original arrangement of blast netting, which lacked any peep-holes for passengers and was also applied to both halves of opening windows rather than the bottom half only, as became the practice later. In this case, the route number stencil is still situated in its pre-war position on the staircase panel.
Malcolm Papes collection

Fifty-four of the LTs equipped with Wilson preselective gearboxes and fluid transmission had petrol engines which they retained until they were withdrawn. All were concentrated at Plumstead garage whose LT 1346 is seen in Regent Street, still with full blind displays, in early wartime.
Alan B. Cross

Chassis:	AEC Renown 663 (LT 1137: 664).
Engine:	AEC A145 6-cylinder 7.4 litre 130 bhp petrol (code 1, 1/2, 3 or 6LT; AEC A171 6-cylinder 7.7 litre 95 bhp oil (LT 21); Gardner 6LW 6-cylinder oil (LT 741, 1417–1426†); AEC A161, A165 or A180 6-cylinder 8.8 litre 130 bhp oil (remainder).
Transmission:	AEC D124 4 speed crash; or Daimler D128 4-speed direct selection pre-selective with fluid flywheel (codes 3, 6 or 8LT).
Bodywork:	LGOC (Chiswick), Park Royal, Strachan or Short Bros.
Capacity:	H30/24RO (LT 1); H32/28RO (2–150*); H33/23R (151–740, 742–949); H34/26R (741, 950–999, 1204–1426)
L.T. chassis code:	1LT (LT 1), 1/2LT (LT 2–20, 22–150); 3LT (LT 271, 401, 451, 469, 470, 571, 573, 580, 582, 588, 591–593, 649, 651, 652, 658, 659, 662, 786, 798, 827, 909, 914); 4LT (LT 191–199, 590, 643, 750–768, 948, 949; 6LT: 964, 1235–1238, 1330–1354); 7LT: (LT 1375–1404); 8LT (LT 1355–1374); 9LT (LT 741, 1417–1426); 10LT (LT 1405–1416); 11LT (LT 950–963, 965–999, 1204–1234, 1239–1329); 12 or 1/12LT (remainder, except 1137 – 1/1LTL).
L.T. Body codes:	LT1 (LT 1); LT2 or 2/1 (LT 2–150*); LT3/1, 3/3, 5/3, 5/5, 5/6, 5/7, 5/8 (LT 151–740, 742–949); LT6/2, 6/3, 6/4, 6/5 (LT 741, 950–999, 1204–1426); LTL2 (LT 1137).
Built:	1929–1932
Number built:	1227
Number in stock:	1.1.40: 1223; 31.12.45: 1203

*LT 21 was fitted with an enclosed staircase LT3/1 body in March 1940 and LT 26 was similarly rebodied with an LT5/8, in August 1945.

†LT 1417 exchanged its Gardner engine for an AEC unit in June 1941. It was recoded 1/7LT6/5.

LT		Date out of stock	LT		Date out of stock	LT		Date out of stock
1	UU6611		69	GH3798		137	GH8034	
2	UU6666		70	GH3834		138	GH8026	
3	UU6667		71	GH3793		139	GH8031	
4	GC3917		72	GH3841		140	GH8035	
5	UU6685		73	GH606		141	GH8040	
6	UU6668		74	GH3795		142	GH8029	
7	UU6669		75	GH638		143	GH8032	
8	GC3904		76	GH3836		144	GH8042	
9	UU6670		77	GH3796		145	GH8037	
10	UU6671		78	GH3866		146	GH8038	
11	GC3905		79	GH3837		147	GH8036	
12	UU6678		80	GH3850		148	GH8045	
13	GC3902		81	GH3838		149	GH8043	
14	GC3920		82	GH605		150	GH8044	
15	UU6686		83	GH3846		151	GK3161	
16	UU6680		84	GH3843		152	GK3162	
17	UU6688		85	GF7275		153	GK3167	
18	GC3906		86	GH608		154	GK3165	15.8.44 b
19	UU6676		87	GH3840		155	GK3168	
20	GC3914		88	GH8013		156	GK3170	
21	GC3922		89	GH3871		157	GK3163	
22	GC3923		90	GH3877		158	GK3159	
23	GC3915		91	GH3835		159	GK3160	
24	GC3924		92	GH3869		160	GK3169	
25	GC3925		93	GH3875		161	GK3164	
26	UU6681		94	GH3870		162	GK5314	
27	GC3926		95	GH3842		163	GK5317	
28	UU6682		96	GH3867		164	GK5322	
29	UU6672		97	GH3868		165	GK5323	
30	UU6673		98	GH3847		166	GK5313	
31	UU6679		99	GH3849		167	GK5320	
32	UU6677		100	GH3844		168	GK5326	
33	UU6675		101	GH3845		169	GK5327	
34	UU6674		102	GH8021		170	GK5316	
35	UU6683		103	GH8007		171	GK5325	
36	GC3921		104	GH3874		172	GK5319	15.8.44 b
37	UU6687		105	GH8019		173	GK5318	
38	GC3901		106	GH3851		174	GK5315	
39	GC3903		107	GH3848		175	GK5321	
40	GC3907		108	GH8008		176	GK5324	
41	UU6684		109	GH3858		177	GK5353	
42	GC3916		110	GH610		178	GK5355	
43	GC3919		111	GH8018		179	GK5352	
44	GC3908		112	GH3876		180	GK5371	
45	GC3913		113	GH3852		181	GK5354	
46	GC3910		114	GH8011		182	GK5366	
47	GC3909		115	GH3859		183	GK5341	
48	GC3911		116	GH3872		184	GK5367	17.8.44 b
49	GC3912		117	GH3863		185	GK5331	
50	GC3918		118	GH3860		186	GK5351	
51	GF7271		119	GH8041		187	GK5340	
52	GH609		120	GH3873		188	GK5339	
53	GF7272		121	GH8009		189	GK5356	
54	GH3799		122	GH8010		190	GK5365	
55	GH640		123	GH8030		191	GK5466	
56	GH3839		124	GH8028		192	GN2067	
57	GH607		125	GH8016		193	GN2172	
58	GH604		126	GH8033		194	GN2054	
59	GH3797		127	GH8017		195	GN2042	
60	GH3832		128	GH8014		196	GN2066	
61	GF7273		129	GH8027		197	GN2119	
62	GF7274		130	GH8012		198	GN2125	
63	GH3833		131	GH8039		199	GK5465	
64	GH3831		132	GH8015		200	GK5428	4.8.44 b
65	GH639		133	GH8022		201	GK5431	
66	GH3794		134	GH8023		202	GK5416	
67	GH3830		135	GH8024		203	GK5417	
68	GH637		136	GH8025		204	GK5409	

b Destroyed by bombing

LT		Date out of stock	LT		Date out of stock	LT		Date out of stock
205	GK5459		273	GN2084		341	GN4627	
206	GK5457		274	GN2100		342	GN4652	
207	GK5427		275	GN2091		343	GN4663	
208	GK5458		276	GN2124		344	GN4658	
209	GK5437		277	GN2129		345	GN4657	
210	GK5462		278	GN2102		346	GN4630	
211	GK5432		279	GN2118		347	GN4617	
212	GK5429		280	GN2122		348	GN4628	
213	GK5436		281	GN2121		349	GN4660	
214	GK5446		282	GN2099		350	GN4665	
215	GK5430		283	GN2120		351	GN4687	
216	GN2139		284	GN2137		352	GK3198	
217	GK5480		285	GN2126		353	GN4676	
218	GK5463		286	GN2133		354	GN4686	
219	GK5464		287	GN2134		355	GN4691	
220	GK5445		288	GN2132		356	GH8084	
221	GK5478		289	GN2127		357	GN4664	
222	GK5454		290	GN2141		358	GN4661	
223	GK5433		291	GN2140		359	GN4678	
224	GN2083	3.8.44 b	292	GN2131		360	GK3197	
225	GN2043		293	GN2151		361	GO619	
226	GK5484		294	GN2135		362	GN4690	
227	GN2049		295	GN2130		363	GN4666	10.8.44 b
228	GN2012		296	GN2138		364	GK3200	
229	GN2117		297	GN2152	17.8.44 b	365	GN4706	
230	GK5485		298	GN2144		366	GN4688	
231	GN2047		299	GN2143		367	GK5500	
232	GN2045		300	GN2136	10.8.44 b	368	GK3199	
233	GN2013		301	GN2142		369	GH8085	
234	GN2014		302	GN2148		370	GN4679	
235	GN2050		303	GN2158		371	GN4680	
236	GN2040		304	GN2186		372	GN4681	
237	GN2046		305	GN2164		373	GN4689	
238	GN2051		306	GN2150		374	GN4710	
239	GN2038		307	GN2159		375	GN4711	
240	GN2044		308	GN2147		376	GN4735	
241	GN2041		309	GN2192		377	GO675	
242	GN2052		310	GN2149		378	GN4703	
243	GN2048		311	GN2185		379	GN4716	
244	GN2055		312	GN2165		380	GN4705	
245	GN2062		313	GN2195		381	GN4712	
246	GN2057		314	GN2171		382	GN4717	
247	GN2053		315	GN2166		383	GN4718	
248	GN2074		316	GN2169		384	GN4702	
249	GN2061		317	GN2157		385	GN4704	
250	GN2073		318	GN2167		386	GN4719	
251	GN2058		319	GN2170		387	GN4720	
252	GN2022		320	GN2184		388	GN4787	
253	GN2065		321	GN2168		389	GO604	
254	GN2056	3.8.44 b	322	GN2196		390	GN4713	
255	GN2060		323	GN2193		391	GN4709	
256	GN2059		324	GN2194		392	GN4729	
257	GN2071		325	GN2190		393	GN4708	
258	GN2070		326	GN4662		394	GN4714	
259	GN2072		327	GN4616		395	GN4747	
260	GN2063		328	GN4685		396	GN4724	
261	GN2082		329	GN4615		397	GO633	
262	GN2064		330	GN4667		398	GN4721	
263	GN2077		331	GN4629		399	GN4727	
264	GN2078		332	GN4656		400	GN4743	
265	GN2092		333	GN4655	4.8.44 b	401	GN4736	
266	GN2088		334	GN2197		402	GN4753	
267	GN2085		335	GN4654		403	GO679	
268	GN2076		336	GN4677		404	GN4723	
269	GN2081		337	GN4653		405	GN4744	
270	GN2123		338	GN4618		406	GN4722	
271	GN2101		339	GN4659		407	GN4728	
272	GN2087		340	GN4626		408	GO632	

b Destroyed by bombing

LT		Date out of stock	LT		Date out of stock	LT		Date out of stock
409	GN4799		477	GO7122		545	GP3502	
410	GN4748		478	GO7140		546	GP3501	
411	GN4764		479	GO7130		547	GP3504	
412	GN4752		480	GO7133		548	GP3488	
413	GN4781		481	GO7137		549	GP3520	
414	GN4749		482	GO7138		550	GP3530	
415	GO620		483	GO7139		551	GP3519	
416	GN4745		484	GO7143		552	GP3505	
417	GN4737	21.8.44 b	485	GO7168		553	GP3495	
418	GO621		486	GO5194		554	GP3494	
419	GO622		487	GO7101		555	GP3486	
420	GN4750		488	GO7170		556	GP3506	
421	GO623		489	GO7176		557	GP3510	
422	GN4751		490	GO7198		558	GP3508	
423	GN4778		491	GO7174		559	GP3509	
424	GN4779		492	GO7169		560	GP3522	
425	GN4746		493	GO7175		561	GP3516	
426	GO608		494	GO7187		562	GP3511	
427	GN4774		495	GO7199		563	GP3518	
428	GO609		496	GO7190		564	GP3517	
429	GO612		497	GO7196		565	GP3531	
430	GO611		498	GO7195		566	GP3507	
431	GN4782		499	GO7194		567	GP3532	
432	GN4800		500	GO7188		568	GP3529	
433	GO624		501	GO7197		569	GP3524	
434	GO613		502	GO7189		570	GP3523	
435	GO674		503	GP3411		571	GP3515	
436	GO683	4.8.44 b	504	GO7191		572	GP3521	
437	GO694		505	GP3416		573	GP3535	
438	GO676		506	GP3419		574	GP3534	
439	GO7124		507	GP3444		575	GP3536	
440	GO691		508	GP3413		576	GP3539	
441	GO690		509	GP3417		577	GP3540	
442	GO682		510	GP3412		578	GP3537	
443	GO677		511	GP3418		579	GP3538	
444	GO681		512	GP3446		580	GP3550	
445	GO680		513	GP3447		581	GP3556	
446	GO693		514	GP3452		582	GP3547	
447	GO692		515	GP3453		583	GP3533	
448	GO7193		516	GP3445		584	GP3544	
449	GO5117		517	GP3442		585	GP3541	
450	GO5154		518	GP3450		586	GP3542	
451	GO5119		519	GP3441		587	GP3545	
452	GO5118		520	GP3451		588	GP3543	
453	GO5120		521	GP3440		589	GP3554	
454	GO5126		522	GP3459		590	GP3576	
455	GO5115		523	GP3467		591	GP3560	
456	GO5135		524	GP3471		592	GT5036	
457	GO5116		525	GP3460		593	GP3546	
458	GO5155		526	GP3477		594	GT7419	
459	GO5147		527	GP3472		595	GP3553	
460	GO5157		528	GP3478		596	GP3552	
461	GO5153	10.8.44 b	529	GP3458		597	GP3549	
462	GO5168		530	GP3474		598	GP3551	
463	GO5156		531	GP3461		599	GP3548	
464	GO5158		532	GP3462		600	GP3558	
465	GO5179		533	GP3468		601	GP3555	
466	GO5184		534	GP3469		602	GP3567	
467	GO5183		535	GP3473		603	GP3559	
468	GO7127		536	GP3466		604	GP3557	
469	GO7123		537	GP3479		605	GP3564	
470	GO7134		538	GP3470		606	GP3561	
471	GO7111		539	GP3493		607	GP3566	
472	GO7112		540	GP3496		608	GP3562	
473	GO7126		541	GP3487		609	GP3563	
474	GO7132		542	GP3489		610	GP3577	
475	GO7131		543	GP3503		611	GP3565	
476	GO7113		544	GP3492		612	GP3568	

b Destroyed by bombing

LT		Date out of stock	LT		Date out of stock	LT		Date out of stock
613	GP3570		681	GT5093		749	GT5181	
614	GP3572		682	GT5096		750	GT5144	
615	GP3573		683	GT5097		751	GT5169	
616	GP3589		684	GT5092		752	GT7467	
617	GP3571		685	GT5105		753	GT7462	
618	GP3569		686	GT5103		754	GT7466	
619	GP3574		687	GT5104		755	GT7478	
620	GP3584		688	GT5106		756	GT7479	
621	GP3588		689	GT5114		757	GT7480	
622	GP3575		690	GT5164		758	GT7481	
623	GP3583		691	GT5119		759	GT7497	
624	GP3582		692	GT5126		760	GT7536	
625	GP3578		693	GT5116		761	GT7562	
626	GP3579		694	GT5115		762	GT7537	
627	GP3586		695	GT5117		763	GT7522	
628	GP3581		696	GT5146		764	GT7563	
629	GP3580		697	GT5121		765	GT7582	
630	GP3585		698	GT5122		766	GT7590	
631	GP3594		699	GT5118		767	GT7585	
632	GP3587		700	GT5123		768	GW5837	
633	GP3590		701	GT5124	21.8.44 b	769	GT5172	
634	GP3592		702	GT5125		770	GT5187	
635	GP3597		703	GT5134		771	GT5179	
636	GP3591		704	GT5127		772	GT5178	
637	GP3593		705	GT5129		773	GT5185	
638	GP3596		706	GT5128		774	GT7404	
639	GP3595		707	GT5131		775	GT5186	
640	GP3598		708	GT5132		776	GT5184	
641	GP3599		709	GT5130		777	GT7420	
642	GT5009		710	GT5133		778	GT5193	
643	GT5012		711	GT5138		779	GT5192	
644	GT5010		712	GT5168		780	GT5190	
645	GT5011		713	GT5140		781	GT5191	
646	GT5017		714	GT5141		782	GT7424	
647	GT5024		715	GT5137		783	GT7402	
648	GT5025		716	GT5139		784	GT7425	
649	GT5018		717	GT5143		785	GT7451	
650	GT5021		718	GT5142		786	GT5195	
651	GT5019		719	GT5147		787	GT5199	
652	GT5020		720	GT5163		788	GT7410	
653	GT5037		721	GT5158		789	GT5200	
654	GT5026		722	GT5194		790	GT7489	
655	GT5023		723	GT5148		791	GT5198	
656	GT5035		724	GT5149		792	GT5197	
657	GT5038		725	GT5150		793	GT7408	3.8.44 b
658	GT5041		726	GT5151		794	GT7403	
659	GT5039		727	GT5160		795	GT7407	
660	GT5049		728	GT5156		796	GT7405	
661	GT5050		729	GT5155		797	GT7401	
662	GT5042		730	GT5152		798	GT7412	
663	GT5040		731	GT5154		799	GT7406	
664	GT5043		732	GT5159	21.8.44 b	800	GT7411	
665	GT5051		733	GT5162		801	GT7415	
666	GT5048		734	GT5174		802	GT7418	
667	GT5063		735	GT5157	21.8.44 b	803	GT7445	
668	GT5055		736	GT5161		804	GT7409	
669	GT5056		737	GT5196		805	GT7517	
670	GT5058		738	GT5170		806	GT7414	
671	GT5065		739	GT5180		807	GT7416	
672	GT5057		740	GT5165		808	GT7413	
673	GT7586		741	GT5167		809	GT7417	
674	GT5066		742	GT5166		810	GT7465	
675	GT5064		743	GT5173		811	GT7434	
676	GT5073		744	GT5171		812	GT7447	
677	GT5089		745	GT5177		813	GT7427	
678	GT5081		746	GT5182		814	GT7450	
679	GT5082		747	GT5175		815	GT7448	
680	GT5091		748	GT5176		816	GT7449	

b Destroyed by bombing

LT		Date out of stock	LT		Date out of stock	LT		Date out of stock
817	GT7433		885	GT7535		953	GW5825	
818	GT7428		886	GT7501		954	GT7593	
819	GT7471		887	GT7559		955	GT7587	
820	GT7430		888	GT7542		956	GT7597	
821	GT7463		889	GT7556		957	GW5839	
822	GT7426		890	GT7511		958	GT7591	
823	GT7459		891	GT7512		959	GT7595	
824	GT7429		892	GT7515		960	GT7599	
825	GT7485		893	GT7503		961	GW5852	
826	GT7461		894	GT7502		962	GW5840	
827	GT7432		895	GT7507		963	GW5832	
828	GT7435		896	GT7505		964	GT7588	
829	GT7460		897	GT7506		965	GW5822	
830	GT7564		898	GT7504		966	GT7592	
831	GT7472		899	GT7510		967	GT7594	
832	GT7436		900	GT7553		968	GT7598	
833	GT7453		901	GT7508		969	GT7600	
834	GT7458		902	GT7521		970	GW5831	
835	GT7437		903	GT7527		971	GW5821	
836	GT7431		904	GT7523		972	GW5845	
837	GT7452		905	GT7524		973	GW5857	
838	GT7438		906	GT7531		974	GW5860	
839	GT7548	17.8.44 b	907	GT7558		975	GW5841	
840	GT7444		908	GT7526		976	GW5856	
841	GT7500		909	GT7529		977	GW5844	
842	GT7442		910	GW5824		978	GW5843	
843	GT7483		911	GT7533		979	GW5848	
844	GT7547		912	GT7540		980	GT7596	
845	GT7496		913	GT7525		981	GW5830	
846	GT7468		914	GT7550		982	GW5826	
847	GT7443		915	GT7520		983	GW5838	
848	GT7454		916	GT7532		984	GW5847	
849	GT7484	3.8.44 b	917	GT7543		985	GW5854	
850	GT7457		918	GT7539		986	GW5827	
851	GT7455		919	GT7530		987	GW5823	
852	GT7456		920	GT7528		988	GW5855	
853	GT7514		921	GT7560		989	GW5851	
854	GT7476		922	GT7538		990	GW5834	
855	GT7469		923	GT7551		991	GW5833	
856	GT7482	3.8.44 b	924	GT7544		992	GW5842	
857	GT7473		925	GT7546		993	GW5836	
858	GT7464		926	GT7565		994	GW5861	
859	GT7470		927	GT7561		995	GW5897	
860	GT7488		928	GT7554		996	GW5876	
861	GT7499		929	GT7549		997	GW5835	
862	GT7474		930	GT7555		998	GW5888	
863	GT7475		931	GT7579		999	GW5859	
864	GT7492		932	GT7583		1137	GP3456	
865	GT7518		933	GT7569		1204	GW5870	
866	GT7487		934	GT7573		1205	GW5853	
867	GT7552		935	GT7584		1206	GW5849	
868	GT7495		936	GT7576		1207	GW5892	
869	GT7589		937	GT7567		1208	GW5867	
870	GT7486		938	GT7568		1209	GW5894	
871	GT7519		939	GT7571		1210	GW5865	
872	GT7493		940	GT7572		1211	GX5212	
873	GT7516		941	GT7570		1212	GW5850	
874	GT7557		942	GT7575		1213	GW5866	
875	GT7545		943	GT7577		1214	GW5877	
876	GT7494		944	GT7581		1215	GW5864	
877	GT7513		945	GT7574		1216	GW5863	
878	GT7491		946	GT7580		1217	GW5880	
879	GT7541		947	GT7578		1218	GW5887	
880	GT7490		948	GW5829		1219	GW5873	
881	GT7509		949	GW5900		1220	GW5872	
882	GT7498		950	GW5846		1221	GW5885	
883	GT7566		951	GW5828		1222	GW5886	
884	GT7534		952	GW5858		1223	GW5884	

b destroyed by bombing

LT		LT		LT	
1224	GW5906	1292	GX5222	1360	GX5358
1225	GW5915	1293	GX5259	1361	GX5359
1226	GW5903	1294	GX5224	1362	GX5360
1227	GW5911	1295	GX5232	1363	GX5361
1228	GW5913	1296	GX5228	1364	GX5362
1229	GW5910	1297	GX5229	1365	GX5363
1230	GW5898	1298	GX5234	1366	GX5364
1231	GW5893	1299	GX5233	1367	GX5365
1232	GW5862	1300	GX5231	1368	GX5366
1233	GW5869	1301	GX5242	1369	GX5367
1234	GW5883	1302	GX5240	1370	GX5368
1235	GW5879	1303	GX5235	1371	GX5369
1236	GW5874	1304	GX5262	1372	GX5370
1237	GW5868	1305	GX5255	1373	GX5371
1238	GW5871	1306	GX5243	1374	GX5372
1239	GW5896	1307	GX5253	1375	GX5294
1240	GW5908	1308	GX5248	1376	GX5284
1241	GW5875	1309	GX5239	1377	GX5283
1242	GW5912	1310	GX5247	1378	GX5280
1243	GW5878	1311	GX5257	1379	GX5289
1244	GW5881	1312	GX5250	1380	GX5312
1245	GW5895	1313	GX5261	1381	GX5296
1246	GW5907	1314	GX5251	1382	GX5295
1247	GW5889	1315	GX5246	1383	GX5341
1248	GW5882	1316	GX5252	1384	GX5298
1249	GX5202	1317	GX5254	1385	GX5300
1250	GW5904	1318	GX5249	1386	GX5297
1251	GW5909	1319	GX5256	1387	GX5306
1252	GX5220	1320	GX5260	1388	GX5307
1253	GW5920	1321	GX5263	1389	GX5309
1254	GW5901	1322	GX5264	1390	GX5313
1255	GW5899	1323	GX5265	1391	GX5339
1256	GX5201	1324	GX5258	1392	GX5308
1257	GW5917	1325	GX5266	1393	GX5340
1258	GW5919	1326	GX5268	1394	GX5342
1259	GW5905	1327	GX5272	1395	GX5343
1260	GX5203	1328	GX5269	1396	GX5344
1261	GW5902	1329	GX5267	1397	GX5345
1262	GX5216	1330	GX5299	1398	GX5346
1263	GX5206	1331	GX5270	1399	GX5347
1264	GX5221	1332	GX5293	1400	GX5348
1265	GW5918	1333	GX5275	1401	GX5349
1266	GW5914	1334	GX5274	1402	GX5350
1267	GX5244	1335	GX5292	1403	GX5351
1268	GW5916	1336	GX5271	1404	GX5352
1269	GX5241	1337	GX5276	1405	GX5373
1270	GX5226	1338	GX5281	1406	GX5374
1271	GX5204	1339	GX5273	1407	GX5375
1272	GX5236	1340	GX5278	1408	GX5376
1273	GX5211	1341	GX5279	1409	GX5377
1274	GX5237	1342	GX5286	1410	GX5378
1275	GX5217	1343	GX5303	1411	GX5379
1276	GX5219	1344	GX5277	1412	GX5380
1277	GX5213	1345	GX5285	1413	GX5381
1278	GX5230	1346	GX5282	1414	GX5382
1279	GX5210	1347	GX5287	1415	GX5383
1280	GX5205	1348	GX5288	1416	GX5384
1281	GX5225	1349	GX5301	1417	GX5385
1282	GX5207	1350	GX5311	1418	GX5386
1283	GX5227	1351	GX5310	1419	GX5387
1284	GX5208	1352	GX5305	1420	GX5388
1285	GX5245	1353	GX5302	1421	GX5389
1286	GX5214	1354	GX5304	1422	GX5390
1287	GX5209	1355	GX5353	1423	GX5391
1288	GX5238	1356	GX5354	1424	GX5392
1289	GX5218	1357	GX5355	1425	GX5393
1290	GX5223	1358	GX5356	1426	GX5394
1291	GX5215	1359	GX5357		

ST

The ST class, based on the AEC Regent 661 chassis, was introduced by the LGOC at the end of 1929, following trial operation of a prototype (which later became ST 1139) by its subsidiaries East Surrey Traction Co. Ltd and Autocar Ltd. The standard STs, which entered service in 1930/31, were the first LGOC production buses to have an enclosed staircase and platform and a total of 906 more or less identical buses was built, including those supplied to East Surrey and the National Omnibus & Transport Co. to operate on behalf of General. ST 1 was built with a square cab of the type used on the T1s and LT 1–50, and this was repeated on forty-six bodies by Ransomes Sims and Jefferies of Ipswich supplied to East Surrey, which became ST 1085–1088/1091–1132 when the Country Bus fleet was numbered in 1935 (coded ST9). The body design used on ST 1 was continued on a further 858 vehicles but with a rounded rather than square cab, which was effectively a forty-nine seat shortened version of the LT3 body (ST 2–168, 170–836, except for the six lowbridge buses; coded ST1/1, 2 or 2/1, and 1040–1069; coded ST9) version of the LT3. One body in this series was built by Metro-Cammell using their patented metal framework and could be distinguished from the rest by its smoother side panels (coded ST3). By 1940 it was mounted on ST 150. Two other bodies had curved staircases, increasing their capacity to fifty-one seats, although this was later reduced to fifty. By 1940 these were mounted on ST 195 (ST6/1)

The ST1/1 body of ST 182, which differed only internally from the ST2 design, exemplifies the standard ST which was a shorter version of the LT3. The final, diamond-shaped, style of peep-hole in the netting can be seen clearly on ST 182, photographed when on loan to the West Yorkshire Road Car Company. A.D. Packer

and ST 294 (ST6). The last ten ST bodies built by LGOC had their front destination indicators mounted in the cab roof, like the LT5/1s, and were classified ST2/1. The six randomly numbered lowbridge buses supplied to National for operation on route 336 had forty-eight seat bodywork by Short Bros; two similar vehicles were purchased by Amersham & District for their share of the route (ST 1089, 1090; coded ST9/1 and 9/3). The last twenty-three LGOC STs supplied to London General Country Services Ltd in 1932 (ST 1032–1039 and 1070–1084; coded ST4) had a new style of bodywork based on the LT 'Bluebird' design but their capacity was held at forty-eight.

A further 191 short wheelbase Regents purchased by Thomas Tilling Ltd in 1930/31 (ST 837–1027; coded ST7) had open staircases, as did the prototype ST 1139 (ST9) and four others acquired by the LPTB from London Independents in 1933 (ST 1038–1031, coded ST8 and variants). The remaining six STs were acquired from the Lewis Omnibus Co. Ltd of Watford in 1933 (ST 1133–1138) and originally had Short Bros bodywork but by 1940 these had been replaced on ST 1135 by a standard ST2 and on ST 1136 and 1137 by ST1/1 bodies. The remainder were similarly rebodied in 1942.

Apart from fifteen allocated originally to The National Omnibus and Transport Company, ST 1–817, 822–832 and 835–1031 were originally Central Buses, painted red. The remainder were Country Buses but ST 819 and 820 were transferred to Central Buses in 1937 and painted red.

At the beginning of 1940 1,137 of the original 1,138 STs were still in stock but

Otherwise standard STs in the Country Bus fleet retained the smaller indicator boxes fitted when they were new and shared the all-embracing classification ST9 with other highbridge types. ST 1041, seen at Caterham, is still in pre-war livery and retains the glazed staircase panel on its Short Brothers body, the white areas on the mudguards being the only indication that it is not a pre-war scene. Michael Rooum

withdrawal of the open staircase buses had started in the summer of 1939 and, in normal circumstances, the rest of the class would have followed during the next two or three years. The Second World War stalled the replacement programme, allowing the majority of standard STs to survive for up to ten more years, despite the class being dealt a severe blow in the early months of the war when Central Bus services were cut to save fuel. The STs were singled out for mass withdrawal because they were petrol driven and had a low passenger capacity. Over 750 Central Bus STs were delicensed, among them a large number of Tillings which were never again to see London service. The number of red STs required for service by the beginning of 1940 had dropped from the pre-war figure of 932 to 223 and the number of Central Bus garages operating the class had fallen from twenty-one, of which nine had no other double-deckers, to five, all operating exclusively ST double-deckers. There were fewer comparable cuts in the Country Area where, apart from temporary withdrawals early in the war, the ST fleet remained more stable and continued to operate from twelve garages. As Central Bus services slowly recovered during 1940, most returned to service but thereafter the allocation of the class was much more scattered in smaller numbers.

The Tilling STs saw little service in London for the duration of the war. All were delicensed in September 1939, thirty-nine did not run in London again and those which returned to service in 1940 had all been withdrawn again by the autumn of 1941. Most then spent much of the rest of the war on loan to operators outside London, a role in which they were joined from July 1942 onwards by standard STs. Up to 147 Tillings, 155 standard STs, ST 1029 and ST 1139 went to operators of all types: municipalities, companies from most of the main groups and Independents. The quantities varied from one to twenty-nine, the operator of the largest number being Coventry Corporation. Nineteen Tillings (as indicated in fleet list) and ST 1028 went to the Home Guard who converted them to armoured cars, four Tillings (841, 909, 1013, 1014) to the BBC, one (930) to the Ministry of Supply and one Tilling (886) and three others (337, 777, 798) to the Royal Navy. Sixty STs were lost through bombing or machine-gunning, twenty-four at Bull Yard, Peckham (including eighteen Tillings), one at Camberwell, two Tillings at Croydon, four at Elmers End (all Tillings), twenty-seven (all Tillings) at Leyton and two in service.

In anticipation of the need to conserve imported fuels, experiments with gas propulsion had started in September 1939 with ST 1100, which was converted using the Bellay system, the equipment for which was mounted on an extension to the rear frame. ST 1100 reverted to normal in 1940. Further experiments using trailers were carried out on ST 132, 1105, 1119 and 1125 from various dates after September 1939 until April 1941. Between 1942 and 1944, more STs were converted for use with trailers and allocated to a number of garages in both the Central and Country areas. The precise number of conversions is uncertain but at least 151 were done and about another 130 were fitted with towing bars but never used as gas buses. All the converted vehicles were restored to petrol propulsion in August and September 1944.

To help cope with the big increase in passenger traffic in the country area during the war many standard STs were transferred to the Country Bus department and painted green. Between December 1943 and September 1945, five STs were converted for use on the Inter Station bus service by having eight lower deck seats removed to create luggage space; they were also repainted blue and yellow. One more was to follow in 1946.

By the end of 1945 the number of STs owned had been reduced to 1,042 but twenty-seven were still out on loan to other operators and a large number of others were unlicensed.

Ransomes Sims and Jefferies of Ipswich supplied forty-six bodies to East Surrey, based on the drawings of ST 1, hence the square cab which distinguished them from the Short Bros. and Chiswick-built bodies. ST 1131 was photographed at Dunton Green garage while still in essentially pre-war condition. J.F. Parke

There were seven lowbridge forty-seat Short Bros. bodied STs, with sunken gangways down both sides of the upper deck (3/1ST9/1) and an almost identical Strachan bodied example (ST 1090: 3/1ST/3). These buses were normally allocated to route 336 but strayed during the war, in this case to Godstone garage on whose 410 route ST 141B is seen at Bromley North. The diamond-shaped window netting peep-holes on the upper deck are set high to allow for the higher position of the seats but the half-drop windows on both decks have the original smaller oblong holes because they were too shallow for the larger type. D.A. Ruddom collection

This rear view of ST 656, after its conversion to producer gas propulsion, shows clearly the full width platform and the bottom of the straight staircase, both features of standard STs and LTs built between 1929 and 1931. The bracket onto which the trailer was fixed for towing can be seen attached to the underside of the platform, from which point the pipe carrying the gas ran under the bus to the engine. The two vertical coolers at the front of the trailer were later augmented by a third, lying flat across the unit, to meet London County Council Fire Regulations. The Omnibus Society

The Tilling STs saw little London service during the war and were most likely to be found on special or emergency duties, such as tramway replacements. A number of routes had peak hour express sections during the winter of 1940/1941 when ST 852 was photographed in Duke Street Hill (London Bridge Station) on a Saturday midday peak journey on route 47. The Omnibus Society

There were twenty-three Bluebird STs (3ST4), the design being a shortened version of that used on the LTs, but full advantage was not taken of the potential for greater capacity which was held at forty-eight seats, giving a very spacious layout particularly on the upper deck. In this view of ST 1073B, a rear-entrance T can be seen behind, about to overtake. Brian Bunker collection

ST 1138B was still carrying its original Short Bros. body when photographed at Bromley North still in the pre-war livery of two shades of green. These bodies were the highbridge version of the ST9/1s but were given the catch-all Country Bus coding of ST9. ST 1138 received an ST1/1 body in March 1942. Frank Willis

Chassis:	AEC Regent 661		
Engine:	AEC A140 6-cylinder 6.1 litre 95bhp petrol		
Transmission:	AEC D124 4-speed crash		
Bodywork:	LGOC (Chiswick), Short Bros. or Strachan (ST 1–836 – except lowbridge, see below); Thos. Tilling or Dodson (ST 837–1027); Birch (ST 1028, 1031); Dodson (ST 1029, 1030); LGOC (ST 1032–1039, 1070–1084); Short Bros. (ST 136, 140, 141, 157, 162, 163, 1040–1069, 1089, 1139); Ransomes Sims and Jefferies (ST 1085–1088, 1091–1132); Strachan (ST 1090); LGOC (ST 1133–1138).		
Capacity:	L24/24R (ST 136, 140, 141, 157, 162, 163, 1089, 1090); H27/25RO (ST 837–1027); H26/22R (ST 1032–1039, 1070–1084); H27/24RO (ST 1139); H28/23R (ST 294); H27/23R (ST 195); H28/20R (remainder).		
L.T. Chassis code:	1 or 2/1ST (ST 1–836, 1040–1069, 1085–1139, except lowbridge: 3/1ST); 2, 1/2 or 2/2ST (ST 831–1031); 3ST (ST 1032–1039, 1070–84).		
L.T. Body codes:	ST2/1 (ST 9, 77, 190, 213, 244, 246, 374, 707, 773); ST3 (150); ST4 (1032–1039, 1070–1084); ST6 (ST 294); ST6/1 (ST 195); ST7 (ST 837–1027); ST8 (ST 1028–1031); ST9 (ST 107, 111, 116, 129, 132, 135, 143, 152, 159, 818–821, 1040–1069, 1085–1088, 1091–1139); ST9/1 (lowbridge except ST 1090); ST9/3 (ST 1090); ST1/1 or 2 (remainder).		
Built:	1929–1932		
Number built:	1138 (plus one instructional chassis)		
Number in stock:	1.1.40: 1137; 31.12.45: 1042 (plus ST169 – instruction chassis)		

ST		Date out of stock	ST		Date out of stock	ST		Date out of stock
1	UU6614		42	GC3981		83	GF406	
2	GO7154		43	GC3975		84	GC3999	
3	GC3927		44	GC3976		85	GF431	
4	GC3928		45	GC3962		86	GF403	
5	GC3930		46	GC3954		87	GF7203	
6	GC3931		47	GC3963		88	GF410	
7	GC3939		48	GC3964		89	GF418	
8	GC3937		49	GC3967		90	GF417	
9	GC3932		50	GC3965		91	GF469	
10	GC3942		51	GC3980		92	GF414	
11	GC3935		52	GC3985		93	GF422	
12	GC3938		53	GC3982		94	GF487	
13	GC3933		54	GC3977		95	GF462	
14	GC3936		55	GC3978		96	GF443	
15	GC3944		56	GC3979		97	GF484	
16	GC3946		57	GC3986		98	GF407	
17	GC3941		58	GF486		99	GF411	
18	GC3934		59	GC3983		100	GF413	
19	GC3940		60	GC3974		101	GF412	
20	GC3951		61	GC3997		102	GF415	
21	GC3955		62	GF404		103	GF442	
22	GC3945		63	GC3991		104	GF436	
23	GC3943		64	GC3992		105	GF424	
24	GC3947	22.10.40 b	65	GC3993		106	GF437	
25	GC3970		66	GC3984		107	GF425	
26	GC3968		67	GC3988		108	GF426	
27	GC3958		68	GF408		109	GF421	
28	GC3969		69	GC3996		110	GF429	
29	GC3949		70	GF402		111	GF427	
30	GC3966		71	GC3990		112	GF430	
31	GC3973		72	GC3987		113	GF432	
32	GC3960		73	GC3989		114	GF419	
33	GC3956		74	GC3995		115	GF420	
34	GC3948		75	GF423		116	GF428	
35	GC3957		76	GF409		117	GF439	
36	GC3952		77	GF416		118	GF433	
37	GC3950		78	GF467		119	GF472	
38	GC3972		79	GC3998		120	GF434	
39	GC3961		80	GF401		121	GF435	
40	GC3971	29.6.43 s	81	GC3994		122	GF444	
41	GC3959		82	GF405		123	GF478	

b Destroyed by bombing　　　s Converted to service vehicle (on date shown)

ST		Date out of stock	ST		Date out of stock	ST		Date out of stock
124	GF448		192	GF7236		260	GH570	
125	GF451		193	GF7240		261	GJ7966	
126	GF473		194	GF7241		262	GH577	
127	GF7211		195	GF7233		263	GH578	
128	GF7209		196	GF7238		264	GJ7967	
129	GF438		197	GF7239		265	GH579	
130	GF454		198	GF7237		266	GH588	
131	GF447		199	GF7248		267	GH581	
132	GF440		200	GF7243		268	GH582	
133	GF445		201	GF7249		269	GJ7968	
134	GF466		202	GF7244		270	GH591	
135	GF441		203	GF7245		271	GH592	
†136	GF7213		204	GF7247		272	GH593	
137	GF7210		205	GF7246		273	GH594	
138	GF452		206	GF7250		274	GH596	
139	GF7202		207	GF7252		275	GH597	
†140	GF7214		208	GJ7954		276	GH595	
†141	GF7217		209	GJ7955		277	GH598	
142	GF450		210	GJ7953		278	GH599	
143	GF457		211	GK3002		279	GH583	
144	GF477		212	GF7253		280	GF552	
145	GF453		213	GJ7956		281	GF553	
146	GF463		214	GJ7951		282	GF554	
147	GF461		215	GJ7958		283	GF556	
148	GF458		216	GJ7952		284	GJ7969	
149	GF446		217	GH544		285	GF7260	
150	GF465		218	GH547		286	GJ7970	
151	GF7204		219	GH545		287	GF489	
152	GF474		220	GJ7964		288	GH600	
153	GF459		221	GH541		289	GH601	
154	GH3864		222	GH555		290	GH584	
155	GF455		223	GH556		291	GH602	
156	GF449		224	GH546		292	GH585	
†157	GF7201		225	GH548		293	GH589	
158	GF7205		226	GH549		294	GH603	
159	GF475		227	GH550		295	GF7255	
160	GF464		228	GJ7957		296	GF7256	
161	GF460		229	GJ7962		297	GF7257	
†162	GF7218		230	GJ7960		298	GH590	
†163	GF7215		231	GJ7959		299	GF7258	
164	GF456		232	GH543		300	GH586	
165	GF470		233	GJ7963		301	GF7259	
166	GF7212		234	GJ7961		302	GH3878	
167	GF471		235	GH560		303	GH3879	
168	GF468		236	GJ7965		304	GH3880	
169	(instructional chassis)		237	GH542		305	GH3891	
170	GF490		238	GH551		306	GH8006	
171	GF476		239	GH552		307	GH8020	
172	GF7228		240	GH553		308	GH8050	
173	GF485		241	GH557		309	GH8052	
174	GN2075		242	GH554		310	GH8046	
175	GF7206		243	GH569		311	GH8053	
176	GF7219		244	GH567		312	GH8055	
177	GF7223		245	GH558		313	GH8048	
178	GF7224		246	GH559		314	GH8056	
179	GF7225		247	GH561	22.10.40 b	315	GH8047	
180	GF7220		248	GH562		316	GH8054	
181	GF7221		249	GH563		317	GH8057	
182	GF7226		250	GH574		318	GH8064	
183	GF7227		251	GH580		319	GH8060	
184	GF7229		252	GH565		320	GH8051	
185	GF7222		253	GH566		321	GH8059	
186	GF7230		254	GH568		322	GH8058	
187	GF7231		255	GH564		323	GH8063	
188	GF7242		256	GH572		324	GH8062	
189	GF7235		257	GH587		325	GH8069	
190	GF7232		258	GH587		326	GH8067	
191	GF7234		259	GH571		327	GH8066	

b Destroyed by bombing   † Lowbridge body

ST		Date out of stock	ST		Date out of stock	ST		Date out of stock
328	GH8061		396	GK3134		464	GK3056	
329	GH8070		397	GK3063		465	GK5305	
330	GH8065		398	GK3118		466	GK3055	
331	GH8068		399	GK3044		467	GK3091	
332	GH8071		400	GK3030		468	GK5311	
333	GH8075		401	GK3062		469	GK3086	
334	GK3005		402	GK3116		470	GK3141	
335	GH8072		403	GK3065		471	GK5308	
336	GH633		404	GK3052		472	GK3142	
337	GH8074	19.6.43	405	GK3129		473	GK3126	
338	GH635		406	GK3115		474	GK3088	
339	GH8076		407	GK3053		475	GK3103	
340	GK3006		408	GK3064		476	GK3085	
341	GH636		409	GK3145		477	GK3087	
342	GK3008		410	GK3081		478	GK5302	
343	GK3037		411	GK3061		479	GK5303	
344	GH634		412	GK3068		480	GK3093	
345	GK3009		413	GK3089		481	GK5312	
346	GK3012		414	GK3071		482	GK5309	
347	GK3042		415	GK3122		483	GK3106	
348	GK3014		416	GK3096		484	GK3136	
349	GK3001		417	GK3066		485	GK3121	
350	GK3004		418	GK5301		486	GK3104	
351	GK3017		419	GK3137		487	GK3102	
352	GK3018		420	GK3072		488	GK3125	
353	GK3016		421	GK3095		489	GK3153	
354	GK3007		422	GK3074		490	GK3124	
355	GK3031		423	GK3138		491	GK3109	
356	GK3013		424	GK3094		492	GK3143	
357	GK3010		425	GK3097		493	GK5307	
358	GK3021		426	GK3084		494	GK5310	
359	GK3022		427	GK3069		495	GK3146	
360	GK3041		428	GK3107		496	GK3152	
361	GK3015		429	GK3157		497	GK5304	
362	GK3023		430	GK3073		498	GK3131	
363	GH8077		431	GK3158		499	GK3148	
364	GH8078		432	GK3110		500	GK3140	22.10.40 b
365	GK3027		433	GK3098		501	GK5306	
366	GK3019		434	GK3105		502	GF7261	
367	GK3020		435	GK3039		503	GF7262	
368	GK3024		436	GK3156		504	GF7263	
369	GK3033		437	GK3111		505	GF7264	
370	GH8073		438	GK3128		506	GF7265	
371	GK3011		439	GK3154		507	GF7266	
372	GK3032		440	GK3060		508	GF7267	
373	GK3025		441	GK3144		509	GF7268	
374	GK3046		442	GK3113		510	GH3861	
375	GK3155		443	GK3051		511	GH3853	
376	GK3082		444	GK3058		512	GH3854	
377	GK3067		445	GK3112		513	GH3862	
378	GK3035		446	GK3147		514	GH3856	
379	GK3034		447	GK3150		515	GH3855	
380	GK3026		448	GK3127		516	GH3857	
381	GK3043		449	GK3092		517	GH3865	
382	GK3045		450	GK3078		518	GK5330	
383	GK3123		451	GK3077		519	GK5334	
384	GK3038		452	GK3099		520	GK5332	
385	GK3057		453	GK3133		521	GK5329	
386	GK3028		454	GK3080		522	GK5328	
387	GK3120		455	GK3114		523	GK5344	
388	GK3059		456	GK3135		524	GK5335	
389	GK3040		457	GK3130		525	GK5346	
390	GK3083		458	GK3139		526	GK5337	22.10.40 b
391	GK3048		459	GK3117		527	GK5336	
392	GK3119		460	GK3151		528	GK5345	
393	GK3036		461	GK3149		529	GK5350	
394	GK3029		462	GK3054		530	GK5343	
395	GK3047		463	GK3079		531	GK5357	

b Destroyed by bombing

ST		Date out of stock	ST		Date out of stock	ST		Date out of stock
532	GK5349		600	GK5438	22.10.40 b	668	GN4606	
533	GK5362		601	GN4797		669	GN2111	
534	GK5348		602	GK5440		670	GN2095	
535	GK5338		603	GK5439		671	GN4675	
536	GK5347		604	GK5456		672	GN4772	
537	GK5376		605	GK5444		673	GN4773	
538	GK5370		606	GK5448		674	GO603	
539	GK5364		607	GK5452		675	GN4639	
540	GK5363		608	GK5451		676	GN4633	
541	GK5359		609	GK5455		677	GN4605	
542	GK5369		610	GK5449		678	GN2113	
543	GK5360		611	GN4695		679	GN4674	
544	GK5361		612	GK5443		680	GN4760	
545	GK5377	1.9.44 b	613	GK5447		681	GN2182	
546	GK5358		614	GK5450		682	GN4641	
547	GK5375		615	GK5461		683	GN4767	
548	GK5373		616	GK5479		684	GN4766	
549	GK5368		617	GK5481		685	GN4651	
550	GK5374		618	GK5460		686	GK3195	
551	GK5372		619	GK5471		687	GH3808	
552	GK5380		620	GK5469		688	GN2116	
553	GK5393		621	GK5477		689	GN4757	
554	GK5378		622	GK5470		690	GN4786	
555	GK5379		623	GK5476		691	GN4759	
556	GK5395		624	GN2028		692	GN4770	
557	GK5384		625	GN2025		693	GN2183	
558	GK5381		626	GN2009		694	GN4692	
559	GK5391		627	GN2011		695	GN2110	
560	GK5385		628	GK5473		696	GN2181	
561	GK5389		629	GK5472		697	GN2098	
562	GK5382		630	GK5483		698	GN2112	
563	GK5383		631	GN2030		699	GN2162	
564	GK5388		632	GK5468		700	GN2097	
565	GK5392		633	GN2026		701	GN4698	
566	GK5390		634	GK5467		702	GN4696	
567	GK5396		635	GN2032		703	GN4650	
568	GK5394		636	GN2010		704	GN4613	
569	GK5386		637	GN2037	17.8.44 b	705	GN4644	
570	GK5387	1.9.44 b	638	GK5475		706	GN2175	
571	GK5398		639	GN2031		707	GN4622	
572	GK5397		640	GK5474		708	GN4619	
573	GK5402		641	GN2033		709	GN4638	
574	GK5399		642	GK5482		710	GN4611	
575	GK5406		643	GN2029		711	GN2189	
576	GK5401		644	GN2027		712	GN4610	
577	GK5414		645	GN4798		713	GN4607	
578	GK5412		646	GN2036		714	GN2173	
579	GK5418		647	GN2035		715	GH8086	
580	GK5404		648	GK3196		716	GH8087	
581	GK5424		649	GN2039		717	GN4758	
582	GK5419		650	GN4693		718	GN4771	
583	GK5423		651	GN4768		719	GN4634	
584	GK5403		652	GN2096		720	GN2155	
585	GK5407		653	GN2034		721	GN4646	
586	GK5434		654	GN4769		722	GN4645	
587	GK5413		655	GN2114		723	GN4642	
588	GK5405		656	GN4631		724	GH8088	
589	GK5422		657	GN2115	12.3.43 b	725	GN2174	
590	GK5410		658	GN4765		726	GN2154	
591	GK5453		659	GN4754		727	GN4608	
592	GK5420		660	GN4636		728	GN4620	
593	GK5426		661	GN4604		729	GO7183	
594	GK3194		662	GN2160		730	GN4788	
595	GK5435		663	GK3193		731	GN2156	
596	GK5425		664	GN4640		732	GN4609	
597	GN4697		665	GN4632		733	GN2153	
598	GK5421		666	GN4694		734	GN4635	
599	GK5411		667	GN4755		735	GN4621	

b Destroyed by bombing

ST		Date out of stock	ST		Date out of stock	ST		Date out of stock
736	GN4756		804	GO5180		872	GJ2048	
737	GN4668		805	GO5129		873	GJ2049	
738	GN2161		806	GO5137		874	GJ2050	
739	GN2180	6.12.40 b	807	GO5151		875	GJ2051	
740	GN4643		808	GO5142		876	GJ2052	16.12.40 ac
741	GN4612		809	GO5140		877	GJ2053	
742	GN4637		810	GO5148		878	GJ2054	24.4.45 b
743	GN4669		811	GO5150		879	GJ2055	1.9.44 b
744	GN2187		812	GO5189		880	GJ2056	
745	GN2188		813	GO5190		881	GJ2057	
746	GO7110		814	GO5195		882	GJ2058	
747	GO615		815	GO7105		883	GJ2059	
748	GO616		816	GO7106		884	GJ2060	
749	GO602		817	GO7114		885	GJ2061	
750	GO610		818	GN4614		886	GJ2062	14.9.40
751	GO634		819	GH3809		887	GJ2063	
752	GO657		820	GN2163		888	GJ2064	
753	GO652		821	GK3192		889	GJ2065	7.12.40 ac
754	GO653		822	GN2128		890	GJ2066	22.10.40 b
755	GO645		823	GN2093		891	GJ2067	
756	GO5106		824	GN2089		892	GJ2068	11.12.40 ac
757	GO658		825	GN2090		893	GJ2069	10.6.41 b
758	GO663		826	GN2094		894	GJ2070	
759	GO678		827	GN4649		895	GJ2071	10.6.41 b
760	GO659		828	GN4623		896	GJ2072	
761	GO5108		829	GN4624		897	GJ2073	24.4.45 b
762	GO697		830	GN4625		898	GJ2074	1.1.41 ac
763	GO5130		831	GN4670		899	GJ2075	
764	GO662		832	GN4733		900	GJ2076	23.5.45 b
765	GO5109		833	GN4731		901	GJ2077	16.12.40 ac
766	GO5145		834	GN4732		902	GJ2078	28.1.41 ac
767	GO664		835	GN4730		903	GJ2079	7.9.45 b
768	GO660		836	GN4734		904	GJ2080	
769	GO686		837	GJ2013	13.6.45 b	905	GJ2081	
770	GO687		838	GJ2014		906	GJ2082	
771	GO5172		839	GJ2015	12.6.45 b	907	GJ2083	
772	GO5163		840	GJ2016	14.9.40 b	908	GJ2084	6.7.45 b
773	GO696		841	GJ2017	10.5.40	909	GJ2085	10.5.40 b
774	GO5110		842	GJ2018		910	GJ2086	
775	GO695		843	GJ2019		911	GJ2087	10.12.40 ac
776	GO5149		844	GJ2020		912	GJ2088	13.8.45
777	GO5101	18.12.42	845	GJ2021		913	GJ2089	
778	GO5136		846	GJ2022		914	GJ2090	
779	GO5121		847	GJ2023		915	GJ2091	
780	GO5105		848	GJ2024		916	GJ2092	
781	GO5103		849	GJ2025		917	GJ2093	
782	GO5102		850	GJ2026		918	GJ2094	
783	GO5122		851	GJ2027	13.10.45 b	919	GJ2095	4.9.45 b
784	GO5111		852	GJ2028		920	GJ2096	
785	GO5104		853	GJ2029	16.12.40 ac	921	GJ2097	
786	GO5112		854	GJ2030	6.6.45 b	922	GJ2098	
787	GO5128		855	GJ2031		923	GJ2099	24.8.45 b
788	GO5107	22.10.40 b	856	GJ2032		924	GJ2100	18.12.40 ac
789	GO5123		857	GJ2033	19.6.45 b	925	GK1001	
790	GO5133		858	GJ2034		926	GK1002	
791	GO5124		859	GJ2035		927	GK1003	22.10.40 b
792	GO5144		860	GJ2036		928	GK1004	
793	GO5131		861	GJ2037		929	GK1005	
794	GO5143		862	GJ2038	25.5.45 b	930	GK1006	12.7.40
795	GO5139		863	GJ2039		931	GK1007	
796	GO7107		864	GJ2040		932	GK1008	31.5.45 b
797	GO5141		865	GJ2041	1.9.45 s	933	GK1009	
798	GO5164	19.6.43	866	GJ2042		934	GK1010	
799	GO5125		867	GJ2043		935	GK1011	
800	GO5138		868	GJ2044		936	GK1012	
801	GO5134		869	GJ2045	18.5.45 b	937	GK1013	12.1.42 s
802	GO5191		870	GJ2046	1.9.45 s	938	GK1014	22.10.40 b
803	GO5127		871	GJ2047	4.10.45 b	939	GK1015	

b Destroyed by bombing;   ac Converted to armoured car for Home Guard;   s Converted to service vehicle

ST		Date out of stock	ST		Date out of stock	ST		Date out of stock
940	GK1016		1008	GK6284	22.10.40 b	1077	GX5321	
941	GK1017		1009	GK6285		1078	GX5322	
942	GK1018		1010	GK6286	22.10.40 b	1079	GX5323	
943	GK1019	6.12.40 ac	1011	GK6287		1080	JH4646	
944	GK1020		1012	GK6288	1.1.41 ac	1081	JH4647	
945	GK1021		1013	GK6289	10.5.40	1082	JH4648	
946	GK1022		1014	GK6290	10.5.40	1083	JH4649	
947	GK1023		1015	GK6291		1084	JH4650	
948	GK1024	11.12.40 ac	1016	GK6292		1085	KR3886	
949	GK1025		1017	GK6293		1086	KR3892	
950	GK1026	20.8.45 b	1018	GK6294		1087	KR3893	
951	GK1027		1019	GK6295	18.12.40 ac	1088	KR3894	
952	GK1028	6.12.40 ac	1020	GK6296		† 1089	KX4656	
953	GK1029		1021	GK6297	22.10.40 b	† 1090	KX5055	
954	GK1030	28.1.41 ac	1022	GK6298		1091	PG7593	
955	GK1031		1023	GN6225		1092	PG7724	
956	GK1032	3.7.45 b	1024	GP6227		1093	PG7725	
957	GK1033		1025	GP6228		1094	PG7726	
958	GK1034	10.12.40 ac	1026	GP6230		1095	PG7727	
959	GK1035		1027	GP6236		1096	PG7728	
960	GK1036	12.7.45 b	1028	GJ8501	18.12.40 ac	1097	PG7836	
961	GK6237	2.5.45 b	1029	VX7487		1098	PG7963	
962	GK6238		1030	VX7553	22.10.40 b	1099	PG7964	
963	GK6239		1031	GJ3020	22.10.40 b	1100	PG7965	
964	GK6240		1032	APC162		1101	PG7966	
965	GK6241	22.10.40 b	1033	APC163		1102	PG7967	
966	GK6242	7.5.45 b	1034	APC164		1103	PG7968	
967	GK6243	22.10.40 b	1035	APC165		1104	PG7969	
968	GK6244		1036	APC166		1105	PG7970	
969	GK6245		1037	APC168		1106	PG7971	
970	GK6246		1038	APC169		1107	PG7972	
971	GK6247		1039	APC170		1108	PG7973	
972	GK6248		1040	GN4699		1109	PG7974	
973	GK6249	22.10.40 b	1041	GN4707		1110	PG7975	
974	GK6250	22.10.40 b	1042	GN4715		1111	PG7976	
975	GK6251		1043	GN4725		1112	PG7977	
976	GK6252		1044	GN4726		1113	PG7978	
977	GK6253		1045	GN4761		1114	PG7979	
978	GK6254	10.12.40 ac	1046	GN4762		1115	PG7980	
979	GK6255		1047	GN4780		1116	PG7981	
980	GK6256	22.10.40 b	1048	GN4789		1117	PG7982	
981	GK6257		1049	GN4796		1118	PG7983	
982	GK6258		1050	GO635		1119	PG7984	
983	GK6259		1052	GO646		1120	PG7985	
984	GK6260	27.4.45 b	1053	GO647		1121	PG7986	
985	GK6261	2.9.43 s	1054	GO654		1122	PG7987	
986	GK6262	27.4.45 b	1055	GO698		1123	PG7988	
987	GK6263		1056	GO700		1124	PG7989	
988	GK6264		1057	GO5132		1125	PG7990	
989	GK6265		1058	GO5146		1126	PG7991	
990	GK6266	22.10.40 b	1059	GO5152		1127	PG7992	
991	GK6267	22.10.40 b	1060	GO5181		1128	PG7993	
992	GK6268	22.10.40 b	1061	GO5182		1129	PG7994	
993	GK6269		1062	GO5188		1130	PG7995	
994	GK6270		1063	GO5193		1131	PG7996	
995	GK6271	11.4.45 b	1064	GO7108		1132	PG7997	
996	GK6272		1065	GO7109		1133	UR5506	
997	GK6273	21.2.41 ac	1066	GO7115		1134	UR5507	
998	GK6274		1067	GO7136		1135	UR5508	
999	GK6275		1068	GO7156		1136	UR5509	
1000	GK6276	13.4.45 b	1069	GO7157		1137	UR5510	
1001	GK6277	29.9.43 s	1070	GX5314		1138	UR7879	
1002	GK6278	14.5.45 b	1071	GX5315		1139	UU6610	
1003	GK6279	22.10.40 b	1072	GX5316				
1004	GK6280	21.2.41 ac	1073	GX5317				
1005	GK6281		1074	GX5318				
1006	GK6282		1075	GX5319				
1007	GK6283	22.10.40 b	1076	GX5320				

b Destroyed by bombing;   ac Converted to armoured car for Home Guard;   s Converted to service vehicle

STL 19, at the Barclay Road stand in Croydon in the early days of the war, has the original type of headlamp mask with curved hood on the nearside only, the offside lamp having had its bulb removed. The STL1 body was another variant of the basic Bluebird design (though never known as such) which, by projecting the upper deck further forward enabled a capacity of sixty to be obtained on a two-axle bus. On this type, the route number was grouped with the intermediate point and destination blinds at both front and back.
The Omnibus Society

STL

The STL was first introduced by Thomas Tilling Ltd and the London General Omnibus Company in 1932 to take advantage of new Regulations which increased the maximum length of double-deckers from 25ft to 26ft. There were originally eighty Tillings (STL 51–130; coded 8STL4 by LPTB in 1934) and one hundred of the first General design, which was a sixty seater based on the 'Bluebird' LT (STL 1–50, 153–202; 1 or 2STL1). In 1933, the LGOC decided to standardise on a capacity of fifty-six for double-deckers and this cleared the way for an improved design with a sloping front, which was applied to the next four hundred (STL 203–552, 559–608; STL2, 3 and variants). At the end of 1934 this was improved further in the STL5 and later STL11 to produce the classic smoothly curved front profile which was the basic design applied to 1,903 of the class, London Transport's standard double-decker between 1933 and 1939. There were two main variants: the Country Bus department took 139 with doorless front entrances (STL 959–1043, 1056–1059 with Chiswick bodywork, coded STL6; STL 1464–1513 with Weymann metal framed bodywork, STL6/1); and forty had inward sloping roofs for operation through Blackwall Tunnel (scattered numbers, STL13). From October 1936 all standard bodies, on a total of 994 buses, had roof route number boxes (STL12, 14, 16 and variants). Of these, 175 (STL 2014–2188) had metal framed bodywork by Park Royal (STL15). Thirty-nine of the last 132 were painted green, the first new rear entrance buses to be allocated to the Country department.

The Tilling variant of the STL was an upgraded version of their ST with enclosed staircase, the front of the upper deck projected forward over the driver's cab and the skirt panels made deeper to give it a more finished look. The retention of the three window arrangement at the front was anachronistic and combined with the small side windows and cramped blind displays to give the bus a pinched look. STL 94 is at the other end of route 119, Bromley North, in the latter days of the war. W.J. Haynes

All STLs were built on the AEC Regent 661 or 0661 chassis. Apart from an experimental batch of eleven vehicles (STLs 342–352; coded 5STL) all STLs numbered below 609 were originally powered by petrol engines and there was a mixture of crash (6STL) and preselective gearboxes (3, 4, 5 and 7STL). The experiment with STLs 342–352 proved successful and from 1934 onwards the standard specification was for 7.7 litre indirect injection oil engine and preselective gearbox, (9STL and variants). When new in 1938, STL 2513–2515 were powered by the A182 8.8 litre oil engine which developed 130 bhp, the same type as used originally in the first RT chassis when operating as ST 1140. Standard 7.7 litre units were substituted in 1942/1943. The chassis of the last 132 pre-war STLs (2516–2647; 15STL16) had an improved specification including the AEC A173 direct injection oil engine, which extensive trials had shown to be more economical and long lasting than the indirect injection type. The enhanced specification also included flexible engine mountings, automatic brake adjusters and automatic chassis lubrication.

There were twenty-two non-standard pre-war STLs. Twelve (STLs 1044–1055; 11STL7), always known as the 'Godstone' STLs, were lowbridge buses built in 1934 for operation by the Country Bus department on route 410. They had stock Weymann forty-eight seat metal framed bodywork and their chassis differed from standard in having crash gearboxes and the AEC 8.8 litre oil engine. Six were acquired from Independents in 1933. Park Royal-bodied STLs 553–557 (coded 12 or 1/12STL8) were acquired, as open toppers, from Charles H Pickup in 1933 and had been fitted with standard Chiswick-built top decks in 1934. Birch bodied STL 558 (13STL9) came from

E. Brickwood and had a petrol engine and preselective gearbox. Its original open staircase body had been enclosed by Brickwood but was altered back by London Transport, making it the only open staircase STL. Four (STLs 1260–1263; 14STL10) were special short wheelbase models fitted with bodies from DSTs.

In 1939, all petrol engined STLs with preselective transmission, except STL 558, were converted to oil, leaving 283 with petrol engines and crash gearboxes. The flexibly mounted A173 engine was used and they were simultaneously fitted with automatic brake adjusters which brought them close to the same mechanical standard as the 15STLs. They were recoded 16STL18, with variants depending on their original classification. This programme was to have been followed by the conversion of the remaining A171 engines from indirect to direct injection embracing 1,916 STLs, but the outbreak of war delayed the start of work and the programme did not get under way until 1943 and was destined never to be completed.

In 1941 London Transport was authorised by the Ministry of War Transport to build twelve new bodies to replace some of those lost in the Blitz. These were built to resemble the latest pre-war design but to austerity standards, including unlined internal panelling, wooden framed seats and fewer opening windows. They were classified STL17 and all but three were mounted on overhauled standard chassis (STL 258, 259, 635, 1245, 1312, 1331, 2355, 2407, 2621). London Transport was later allocated thirty-four 'unfrozen' Regent chassis (STL 2648–2681; 17STL) for which twenty lowbridge (STL19) and fourteen highbridge (STL17/1) austerity bodies were built at Chiswick. The chassis were standard AEC products with crash gearboxes and none of the refinements usually specified by London Transport. The highbridge bodies were similar to the STL17s but lacked a front route number box and rear indicator display. All of the lowbridge bodies and one of the highbridge version were fitted to standard chassis and eighteen of the new chassis received bodies of various pre-war types from the works float. Three received STL17 bodies (STL 2651, 2657, 2669). The bodies mounted on the 17STLs were painted red when new but all operated exclusively in the Country area. A programme to repaint them green started in January 1944.

The unfrozen STLs went into service between 1st December 1941 and 1st October 1942, twelve to High Wycombe, seventeen to Amersham, four to Watford High Street and one to Godstone. The primary purpose of the High Wycombe and Amersham allocations was to replace single-deckers on routes 353, 362/A and they were the only double-deckers allowed to use Amersham Hill, High Wycombe, for which their transmission made them most suitable. The Watford group later went to Godstone, where they were joined by others from High Wycombe and Amersham, to replace STs on routes 409 and 411, on which their transmission was well suited to the steep climb up Church Hill, Caterham.

Two STLs were modified for use in Pay-As-You-Enter experiments which took place on route 65 between October 1944 and April 1946. STL 1793 was rebuilt in September 1944 with a single central entrance and STL 2284 in August 1945 with separate entrance and exit doors in the first and third bays. In both cases war damaged bodies were used. After March 1945 STL 1793 ran in normal service still in its modified state.

The war had a significant effect on the allocation of STLs. In the early months many were used at unfamiliar garages to cover the withdrawal of the petrol-engined STs and later were allocated on a more permanent basis to replace STs or LTs at various garages. STLs were also transferred from Central Buses to help cope with the substantial increase in demand in the Country Area, up to four hundred being on loan at any one time. From December 1940 the restored Green Line services were converted progressively to double-deck using STLs, at first using existing green buses which were replaced in normal bus service by borrowed red vehicles but later, starting in March 1941, eighty-nine were repainted from red to green for this purpose. A further 158 were repainted for Country Area bus work in 1944 and 1945, making a total of 247, including twenty-nine of the 'sloping-bodied' STL18s and ten 15STL16s.

The 283 petrol-engined STLs with crash gearboxes were omitted from the programme of conversion to oil in 1939, 103 of them being 6STLs, like STL 331. This has an STL3 body with a square route number box, although this is disguised by the black masking paint which has been lined up with the larger box alongside. J.H. Price

In normal circumstances a start would have been made on the withdrawal of the oldest STLs in 1943/1944 but, like the STs and LTs, they were given a reprieve of up to six years and most were still in stock at the end of 1945. The only STL to be withdrawn voluntarily before the end of 1945 was the unique STL 558 which was delicensed and stored in September 1944. Sixty-one STLs, mostly petrol-engined, were lost through enemy action, of which no fewer than fifty-four were destroyed in one incident when Croydon garage was bombed on the night of 10/11th May 1941. In that one night twenty-two Tillings, twenty-two 6STL3, five 1STL1s, four 2STL1 and Pickup STL 554 were destroyed. Apart from another Tilling lost at Elmers End in 1944, the rest were standard oil-engined STLs. The bodies of many other STLs were damaged beyond repair and replaced by spares from the float, giving rise to the appearance of bodies of the 'wrong' type. One of the losses was the Dodson body carried by short-wheelbase STL 1262 which was destroyed in a flying bomb attack at Aldwych in 1944. A standard ST body was substituted but the driver's cab was that of a standard STL. One tunnel body was destroyed, reducing the number to thirty-nine as there was no float for this type, but altogether three of the original STL13s exchanged their tunnel bodies for standard types. The two STL13 bodies released by this were fitted to STLs 834 and 2437. The STLs were subjected to the same wartime modifications and expedients as other classes, including the installation of wooden slatted seats in twenty-nine, five of which were STL6s, between March and September 1944.

Above **In 1939 all STLs with preselective gearboxes numbered below 609 were fitted with new direct-injection oil engines and brought up to date in other respects to make them almost comparable to the latest 15STL. In consequence, they were reclassified and STL 477, having been a 7STL3, became a 2/16STL18. Its body is one of the later style of STL3 with the deeper aperture glass in the route number box masked to give the correct display size. It was one of those drafted into Country Bus service and is seen, still in Central Bus red livery at Bromley North before it was repainted green in February 1945.** W.J. Haynes

London Transport's first standard double-deck design was the STL5, which had less slope than earlier designs but a smoother profile. STL 881 was new in September 1935 and is seen at Oxford Road, Putney. W.J. Haynes

The STL11 body type was similar to the STL5 but could be distinguished readily by the position of the destination indicator box above the route number and intermediate point blinds. STL 1628 was new to Central Buses in October 1936 but is seen at Sevenoaks bus station after its wartime transfer to Country Buses. J.F. Parke

The distinctive metal-framed lowbridge body of 'Godstone' STL 1051B has been painted in the wartime green and white livery, with brown roof. The restricted indicator display on these was usually the same as on standard Country Area STLs, with the route number box still in use, but in this case the masking has allowed the use of an ST type blind. The positioning of the peepholes on the upper deck reveals the position of the staircase well, the diamond in the second bay being at a lower level than the two further back which are aligned for seated passengers. W.J. Haynes

The 'Pickup' STLs (12STL8) were among the most distinctive of the type, combining as they did six-bay Park Royal built lower decks of what were originally open-top bodies, with five bay upper decks built at Chiswick. STL 556 is seen at Telford Avenue in service from Croydon garage on route 133. W.J. Haynes

Of the four short wheelbase 14STL10s, STL 1262 was unique in having the Dodson body originally carried by DST 5, which had been acquired from Redline. The body was destroyed by a V1 bomb whilst on the stand at Aldwych on 30th June 1944 but the chassis was rescued, lengthened and fitted with a standard STL12 body. D.W.K. Jones

STL 1043 was a Chiswick-built forward entrance 10STL6, seating fifty-two, which had been painted in green and white livery but still had full blind displays when photographed at Sutton at Hone. It also still had its original side lights at cantrail level but this arrangement was found to be unsatisfactory in the blackout and they were later replaced by standard fittings on the dash and front bulkhead panels. A.B. Cross

The main points of distinction between the Weymann-bodied STL6/1 and the STL6 were the radiused tops to the front upper deck windows and the position of the destination indicator at the top of the display, the type being based on the STL11 design. STL 1475 is seen towards the end of the war when lighting regulations had been eased and maintenance of the window webbing had already fallen into neglect. W.J. Haynes

The clearances in Blackwall Tunnel determined the profile of the STL13 body type, which had an inward sloping upper deck. STL 1854, seen at Crystal Palace Parade, has a modified style of restricted blind display which fills the whole aperture to allow for a larger route number, but carries no more information than the standard type. Frank Willis

Externally, there was nothing to distinguish an STL12 from an STL14, the two types which reintroduced the roof route number box, the differences being under the skin. STL 2417, a 4/9STL14/1, was one of those drafted into Country Bus service at the beginning of the war and is seen at Godstone garage soon afterwards, still painted red and with the first type of headlamp mask. Its indicator boxes have been masked so that it can be fitted with a blind from an ST, the type normally operated. It was repainted green in June 1941. D.W.K. Jones

STL 2222, a 4/9STL14/1, was fitted out as an example of London Transport's new policy of replacing some glass with metal or wooden panels to overcome the general shortage of glass. This was an extreme example, however, normal practice being to board up fewer windows on each bus. London Transport

Thirty-nine of the final STL design, the 15STL16, were painted green for Country Bus operation but a number were transferred to Green Line duty at Grays when the Z group was re-instated. STL 2612 was only a few months old when photographed at Aldgate and therefore in almost original condition, with its distinctive longer radiator and wheel trim discs, although dressed for blackout operation. STL 2321 alongside is another STL14/1. E.G.P. Masterman

There were only three pure 17STL17s, one being STL 2657. The STL17 body was based on the latest pre-war designs but austerity standards prevailed, including the loss of opening front windows, no panel lining inside the saloons and the use of wooden framed seats. The long slatted radiator showed that these were standard Regents. J.F. Parke

Anti-blast netting as originally fitted to the windows of an STL. The rectangular peep-holes were soon changed to ones of diamond shape seen elsewhere in this book and the practice was adopted of not covering the top halves of opening windows.
London Transport

The lowbridge STL19 bodies were recognisably an STL design and showed little external evidence of the austerity nature of their construction which was more evident inside the saloons. STL 1617, seen at Northwick Park, had been a 4/9STL11 when new in 1936. E.G.P. Masterman

The austerity nature of the STL19 body was shown in the wood-framed seats and unlined side panels. The less intrusive foreshortened type of lamp mask, usually used upstairs, was fitted to the lower decks of lowbridge buses. London Transport

The rear view of the standard STL changed little over the production run, its distinctive features being the upper-deck emergency window, with Y-shaped dividing rail, and the full set of indicator blinds. On the left in Victoria garage, STL 1373 is an STL11, while STL 1944, on the right, is an STL14. Malcolm Papes collection

In September 1944, STL 1793 was converted for use in the 'Pay as You Board' experiments, with seated conductor. It had a single doorway, enclosed by a sliding door, with the conductor seated opposite, alongside the staircase which had been moved to the centre of the body. There was a full width seat across the rear of each saloon, with emergency exit windows above, which enabled the seating capacity to be kept at fifty-six. It is seen at the Argyle Road, Ealing, terminus of route 65. C.F. Klapper

Separate entrance and exit doors were included in the modification of STL 2284 for the PAYB experiments, with the conductor seated on the nearside of the saloon between them. The staircase was also further forward and there were more longitudinal seats. There was a full width seat across the back of the upper deck but the lower deck arrangement was similar to an STL6 with a centrally placed emergency door between two double seats, the total capacity being reduced to fifty-four. London Transport

Chassis:	AEC Regent 661 or 0661	
Engine:	AEC A140 6-cylinder 6.1 litre 95 bhp petrol (STL 1–130, 153–202, 553–558); AEC A145 6-cylinder 7.4 litre 130 bhp petrol (STL 253, 263, 290, 292–341, 353–402); AEC A165 6-cylinder 8.8 litre 130 bhp oil (STL 1044–1055); AEC A182 6-cylinder 8.8 litre 130 bhp oil (STL 2513–2516) AEC A171 (indirect injection) or A173 (direct injection) 6-cylinder 7.7 litre 95 bhp oil (remainder).	
Transmission:	AEC D124 4 speed crash STL (1–130, 153–202, 253, 263, 290, 292–341, 353–402, 553–557, 2648–2681); AEC experimental 4-speed synchromesh (STL 253, 263, 290); or four speed direct selection preselective (D128 Daimler or D132 AEC) with fluid flywheel (remainder).	
Chassis codes:	1STL (STL 1–20, 22–31, 33–41, 43, 45–49); 2STL (STL 32, 153–202); 3STL (STL 50); 1/4STL (STL 253, 263, 290); 5STL (STL 342–352); 6STL (STL 21, 42, 44, 292–341, 353–402); 8STL (STL 51–130); 9, 1/9, 2/9, 3/9, 4/9STL (STL 609–958, 1060–1259, 1264–1463, 1514–2515, except lowbridge); 10 or 1/10STL (STL 959–1043, 1056–1059, 1464–1513); 11STL (STL 1044–1055); 12 or 12/1STL (STL 553–557); 13STL (STL 558); 14STL (STL 1260–1263); 15 or 1/15STL (STL 2516–2647); 16STL (STL 203–252); 1/16STL (STL 254–262, 264–289, 291); 2/16STL (STL 403–552, 559–608); 17STL (STL 2648–2681)	
Bodywork:	LGOC or LPTB (Chiswick) or Park Royal, except: Tilling (STL 51–130); Chiswick/Park Royal (STL 553–557); Dodson (STL 558, 1262); Weymann (STL 1044–1055, 1466–1476, 1478–1513)	
Capacity:	H30/26R except: STL 1–50, 153–202, 2674, 2679 H34/26R; STL 558 H26/24RO; STL 1044–1055 L26/22FD; STL 959–975, 977–992, 994–1000, 1001, 1002, 1004–1043, 1056–1059 H29/23F; STL 1464–1476, 1478–1513 H29/19F; STL13 type Tunnel buses (see fleet list) H30/25R; STL19 lowbridge type (see fleet list) L27/26R.	
Body codes:	STL1 (STL 1–49, 153–202); STL1/1 (STL 50, 2674, 2679); STL2/1 (STL 2664); STL3 (STL 292–341, 353–374, 376–402); STL3/1 (STL 342–352); STL3/2 (STL 253, 263, 290, 375); STL3/3 (STL 2663, 2681); STL3/4 (STL 2675); STL4 (STL 51–130); STL6 (STL 959–974, 976–992, 994–1000, 1002, 1004–1043, 1056–1059); STL6/1 (STL 1464–1476, 1478–1513); STL7 (STL 1044–1055); STL8 (STL 553–558); STL10 (STL 1260–1263); STL13 (tunnel buses – see fleet list); STL17 (after 1942 – STL 258, 259, 1245, 1312, 1331, 2355, 2407, 2621, 2651, 2657, 2669); STL17/1 (STL 932 – after 1942, 2654, 2661, 2665–2668, 2671–2673, 2676–2678, 2680); STL18 (STL 203–252); STL18/1 (STL 254–262, 264–289, 291, 403–552, 559–608); STL19 (Chiswick-built lowbridge – see fleet list); STL5, 5/1, 5/2, 5/3, 11, 11/1, 12, 12/1, 14, 14/1, 14/2, 15, 16, 16/1, 16/2 (standard types – remainder).	
Built:	1932–1942	
Number built (by 31.12.45):	2659;	
Number in stock:	1.1.40: 2625; 31.12.45: 2598	

STL		Date out of stock	STL		Date out of stock	STL		Date out of stock
1	GX5324		13	JJ4337	10.6.41 b	25	JJ4358	
2	JJ4340	10.6.41 b	14	JJ4342		26	JJ4335	10.6.41 b
3	JJ4364		15	JJ4357		27	GX5336	
4	JJ4341		16	GX5330		28	JJ4338	
5	JJ4353		17	GX5399		29	JJ4331	
6	JJ4344		18	GX5329		30	GX5398	
7	JJ4346		19	JJ4366		31	JJ4343	
8	JJ4360		20	GX5328		32	GX5334	10.6.41 b
9	JJ4354		21	JJ4362		33	JJ4359	
10	JJ4361		22	JJ4355		34	JJ4348	
11	GX5400	10.6.41 b	23	GX5335		35	JJ4336	
12	JJ4365		24	JJ4332		36	JJ4345	

b Destroyed by bombing

STL		Date out of stock	STL		Date out of stock	STL		Date out of stock
37	JJ4350		105	JJ6305	10.6.41 b	195	AGX541	
38	JJ4339		106	JJ6306	10.6.41 b	196	AGX534	10.6.41 b
39	JJ4351		107	JJ6307	10.6.41 b	197	AGX538	
40	JJ4352		108	JJ6308		198	AGX537	
41	JJ4347		109	JJ6309		199	AGX543	
42	JJ4371		110	JJ6310	10.6.41 b	200	AGX539	
43	JJ4349		111	AGF821		201	AGX540	
44	JJ4356		112	AGF822	10.6.41 b	202	AGX542	
45	JJ4367		113	AGF823		203	AGX547	
46	JJ4368		114	AGF824		204	AGX557	
47	JJ4372		115	AGF825		205	AGX548	
48	JJ4369		116	AGF826	10.6.41 b	206	AGX552	
49	JJ4370		117	AGF827		207	AGX545	
50	JJ4363		118	AGF828		208	AGX546	
51	YY5351		119	AGF829		209	AGX559	
52	YY5352		120	AGF830	10.6.41 b	210	AGX549	
53	YY5353	10.6.41 b	121	AGF831		211	AGX556	
54	YY5354		122	AGF832		212	AGX554	
55	YY5355		123	AGF833		213	AGX583	
56	YY5356		124	AGF834		214	AGX584	
57	YY5357		125	AGF835		215	AGX558	
58	YY5358		126	AGF836		216	AGX560	
59	YY5359		127	AGF837	10.6.41 b	217	AGX585	
60	YY5360		128	AGF838		218	AGX551	
61	YY5361		129	AGF839	10.6.41 b	219	AGX574	
62	YY5362		130	AGF840	10.6.41 b	220	AGX564	
63	YY5363	4.8.44 b	153	AGX505		221	AGX561	
64	YY5364		154	AGX510		222	AGX563	
65	YY5365		155	AGX513		223	AGX562	
66	YY5366		156	JJ4378	10.6.41 b	224	AGX553	
67	YY5367		157	AGX506		225	AGX555	
68	YY5368		158	AGX501		226	AGX598	
69	YY5369		159	JJ4376		227	AGX588	
70	YY5370		160	AGX503		228	AGX575	
71	YY5371	10.6.41 b	161	AGX550		229	AGX568	
72	YY5372		162	JJ4379		230	AGX571	
73	YY5373		163	AGX509		231	AGX572	
74	YY5374		164	AGX511		232	AGX565	
75	YY5375		165	JJ4377		233	AGX592	
76	YY5376		166	AGX512		234	AGX570	
77	YY5377		167	JJ4380		235	AGX573	
78	YY5378		168	AGX518		236	AGX590	
79	YY5379		169	AGX520		237	AGX576	
80	YY5380		170	AGX508	10.6.41 b	238	AGX597	
81	JJ6281		171	AGX502		239	AGX589	
82	JJ6282	10.6.41 b	172	AGX507		240	AGX582	
83	JJ6283		173	AGX504	10.6.41 b	241	AGX596	
84	JJ6284		174	AGX514		242	AGX566	
85	JJ6285		175	AGX517		243	AGX567	
86	JJ6286		176	AGX515		244	AGX577	
87	JJ6287	10.6.41 b	177	AGX516		245	AGX581	
88	JJ6288	10.6.41 b	178	AGX533		246	AGX580	
89	JJ6289		179	AGX535		247	AGX569	
90	JJ6290		180	AGX522		248	AGX586	
91	JJ6291		181	AGX523		249	AGX593	
92	JJ6292		182	AGX521		250	AGX578	
93	JJ6293		183	AGX519		251	AGX587	
94	JJ6294		184	AGX530		252	AGX579	
95	JJ6295		185	AGX525		253	AUC546	
96	JJ6296	10.6.41 b	186	AGX532		254	AUC512	
97	JJ6297	10.6.41 b	187	AGX524		255	AUC539	
98	JJ6298	10.6.41 b	188	AGX531		256	AUC542	
99	JJ6299	10.6.41 b	189	AGX527		257	AUC548	
100	JJ6300	10.6.41 b	190	AGX529		258	AUC544	
101	JJ6301	10.6.41 b	191	AGX528		259	AUC538	
102	JJ6302		192	AGX544		260	AUC522	
103	JJ6303		193	AGX526		261	AUC513	
104	JJ6304	10.6.41 b	194	AGX536		262	AUC510	

b Destroyed by bombing

STL		Date out of stock	STL		Date out of stock	STL		Date out of stock
263	AUC511		331	AUC599		399	AXM651	
264	AUC507		332	AUC596		400	AXM659	10.6.41 b
265	AGX595		333	AXM677		401	AXM662	
266	AGX591		334	AXM607		402	AXM656	10.6.41 b
267	AUC533		335	AXM601		403	AXM666	
268	AUC518		336	AXM606		404	AXM667	
269	AUC514		337	AXM603		405	AXM655	
270	AGX594		338	AXM602		406	AXM668	
271	AUC519		339	AXM609		407	AXM657	
272	AGX599		340	AXM608	10.6.41 b	408	AXM674	
273	AUC506		341	AXM604		409	AXM663	
274	AUC505		342	AUC557		410	AXM664	
275	AUC537		343	AUC591		411	AXM673	
276	AUC516		344	AUC563		412	AXM675	
277	AUC517		345	AUC581		413	AXM676	
278	AUC524		346	AUC564		414	AXM669	
279	AUC543		347	AUC565		415	AXM665	
280	AUC520		348	AUC582		416	AXM672	
281	AUC525		349	AUC575		417	AXM671	
282	AUC536		350	AUC576		418	AXM685	
283	AUC526		351	AXM613		419	AXM681	
284	AUC547		352	AXM654		420	AXM682	
285	AUC527		353	AXM620		421	AXM684	
286	AUC532		354	AXM624		422	AXM670	
287	AUC541		355	AXM625	10.6.41 b	423	AXM680	
288	AUC540		356	AXM633		424	AXM683	
289	AUC545		357	AXM614		425	AXM678	
290	AUC551		358	AXM611	10.6.41 b	426	AXM679	
291	AUC549		359	AXM621		427	AYV610	
292	AUC550		360	AXM632		428	AXM687	
293	AUC560		361	AXM622		429	AXM688	
294	AUC559		362	AXM615		430	AXM689	
295	AUC556		363	AXM610		431	AYV637	
296	AUC552		364	AXM619	10.6.41 b	432	AXM690	
297	AUC554		365	AXM617		433	AXM691	
298	AUC553		366	AXM638		434	AXM686	
299	AUC555		367	AXM627	10.6.41 b	435	AXM692	
300	AUC561		368	AXM636	10.6.41 b	436	AXM697	
301	AUC558		369	AXM628		437	AYV611	
302	AUC566	10.6.41 b	370	AXM616		438	AYV608	
303	AUC562		371	AXM623		439	AXM696	
304	AUC577		372	AXM618		440	AXM699	
305	AUC578	10.6.41 b	373	AXM629		441	AXM693	
306	AUC569		374	AXM630		442	AXM700	
307	AUC567		375	AXM640		443	AXM695	
308	AUC568		376	AXM641		444	AYV601	
309	AUC579		377	AXM639		445	AXM694	
310	AUC570		378	AXM626	10.6.41 b	446	AYV604	
311	AUC571		379	AXM637		447	AYV602	
312	AUC572		380	AXM634	10.6.41 b	448	AYV607	
313	AUC573		381	AXM635		449	AYV612	
314	AUC574		382	AXM650		450	AYV603	
315	AUC592		383	AXM631		451	AYV605	
316	AUC583		384	AUC521		452	AYV606	
317	AUC586		385	AXM642	10.6.41 b	453	AYV633	
318	AUC585		386	AXM643		454	AYV625	
319	AUC588		387	AXM644		455	AYV619	
320	AUC580		388	AXM645		456	AYV630	
321	AUC600		389	AXM646	10.6.41 b	457	AYV614	
322	AUC589		390	AXM649		458	AYV621	
323	AUC587		391	AXM648	10.6.41 b	459	AYV613	
324	AUC584		392	AXM647	10.6.41 b	460	AYV609	
325	AUC593		393	AXM652	10.6.41 b	461	AYV622	
326	AUC590	10.6.41 b	394	AXM653	10.6.41 b	462	AYV617	
327	AUC594	10.6.41 b	395	AXM698	10.6.41 b	463	AYV642	
328	AUC595	10.6.41 b	396	AXM661		464	AYV620	
329	AUC597		397	AUC598		465	AYV643	
330	AXM658		398	AXM612		466	AYV618	

b Destroyed by bombing

STL		Date out of stock	STL		Date out of stock	STL		Date out of stock
467	AYV641		535	AYV725		603	AYV756	
468	AYV628		536	AYV705		604	AYV762	
469	AYV651		537	AYV706		605	AYV759	
470	AYV644		538	AYV703		606	AYV757	
471	AYV649		539	AYV700		607	AYV761	
472	AYV646		540	AYV695		608	AYV763	
473	AYV624		541	AYV716		609	AYV766	
474	AYV623		542	AYV684		610	AYV772	
475	AYV645		543	AYV696		611	AYV769	
476	AYV627		544	AYV692		612	AYV774	
477	AYV634		545	AYV708		613	AYV770	
478	AYV632		546	AYV693		614	AYV775	
479	AYV652		547	AYV714		615	AYV773	
480	AYV655		548	AYV710		616	AYV779	
481	AYV640		549	AYV699		617	AYV787	
482	AYV626		550	AYV702		618	AYV768	
483	AYV636		551	AYV709		619	AYV767	
484	AYV629		552	AYV715		620	AYV776	
485	AYV639		553	GW1744		621	AYV771	
486	AYV631		554	GW1224	10.6.41 b	622	AYV788	
487	AYV638		555	GW1785		623	AYV783	
488	AYV635		556	GX167		624	BLH702	
489	GY650		557	GY839		625	AYV777	
490	AYV648		558	GW2294		626	AYV780	
491	AYV659		559	AYV750		627	BLH717	
492	AYV665		560	AYV719		628	BLH711	
493	AYV653		561	AYV721		629	AYV789	
494	AYV654		562	AYV727		630	AYV792	
495	AYV647		563	AYV712		631	BLH703	
496	AYV666		564	AYV735		632	AYV781	
497	AYV658		565	AYV718		633	BLH740	
498	AYV670		566	AYV711		634	BLH716	
499	AYV656		567	AYV723		635	AYV785	
500	AYV688		568	AYV726		636	AYV793	
501	AYV678		569	AYV722		637	AYV782	
502	AYV674		570	AYV720		638	AYV778	
503	AYV669		571	AYV732		639	AYV786	
504	AYV675		572	AYV733		640	BLH701	
505	AYV686		573	AYV713		641	BLH738	
506	AYV689		574	AYV724		642	AYV790	
507	AYV690		575	AYV728		643	BLH709	
508	AYV682		576	AYV743		644	AYV784	
509	AYV681		577	AYV741		645	BLH712	
510	AYV697		578	AYV734		646	AYV791	
511	AYV698		579	AYV738		647	BLH705	
512	AYV657		580	AYV729		648	BLH733	
513	AYV683		581	AYV730		649	BLH706	
514	AYV671		582	AYV731		650	BLH708	
515	AYV660		583	AYV739		651	BLH704	
516	AYV661		584	AYV740		652	BLH707	
517	AYV662		585	AYV736		653	BLH710	
518	AYV667		586	AYV760		654	BLH715	
519	AYV663		587	AYV744		655	BLH718	
520	AYV687		588	AYV751		656	BLH719	
521	AYV664		589	AYV753		657	BLH720	
522	AYV694		590	AYV749		658	BLH722	
523	AYV676		591	AYV737		659	BLH723	
524	AYV672		592	AYV752		660	BLH732	
525	AYV668		593	AYV742		661	BLH713	
526	AYV704		594	AYV765		662	BLH714	
527	AYV701		595	AYV747		663	BLH725	
528	AYV707		596	AYV754		664	BLH726	
529	AYV679		597	AYV755		665	BLH741	
530	AYV673		598	AYV748		666	BLH729	
531	AYV685		599	AYV745		667	BLH734	
532	AYV680		600	AYV746		668	BLH721	
533	AYV677		601	AYV764		669	BLH727	
534	AYV691		602	AYV758		670	BLH760	

b Destroyed by bombing   s Converted to service vehicle

STL		Date out of stock	STL		Date out of stock	STL		Date out of stock
671	BLH731		739	BXD405		807	BXD470	
672	BLH730		740	BXD403		808	BXD489	
673	BLH736		741	BXD418		809	BXD485	
674	BLH728		742	BXD451		810	BXD471	
675	BLH735		743	BXD416		811	BXD486	
676	BLH724		744	BXD417		812	BXD511	
677	BLH745		745	DGX260	26.8.44 b	813	BXD487	
678	BLH771		746	BXD413		814	BXD477	
679	BLH739		747	BXD412		815	CGJ77	
680	BLH742		748	BXD406		816	BXD493	
681	BLH743		749	BXD409		817	BXD472	
682	BLH737		750	BXD411		818	BXD507	
683	BLH746		751	BXD415		819	BXD478	
684	BLH747		752	BXD407		820	BXD494	
685	BLH748		753	BXD410		821	BXD481	
686	BLH749		754	BXD420		822	BXD510	
687	BLH744		755	BXD422		823	BXD475	
688	BLH764		756	BXD419		824	BXD495	
689	BLH750		757	BXD424		825	BXD496	
690	BLH759		758	BXD423		826	BXD479	
691	BLH752		759	BXD425		827	BXD482	
692	BLH754		760	BXD441		828	BXD483	
693	BLH751		761	BXD455		829	BXD497	
694	BLH753		762	BXD426		830	BXD488	
695	BLH756		763	BXD431		831	BXD518	
696	BLH758		764	BXD443		832	BXD579	
697	BLH757		765	BXD449		833	BXD509	
698	BLH755		766	BXD444		tt 834	BXD499	
699	BLH761		767	BXD437		835	BXD490	
700	BLH768		768	BXD445		836	BXD505	
701	BLH765		769	BXD473		837	BXD515	
702	BLH763		770	BXD466		838	BXD610	
703	BLH762		771	BXD442		839	BXD585	
704	BLH770		772	BXD434		840	BXD491	
705	BLH766		773	BXD432		841	BXD492	
706	BLH767		774	BXD436		842	BXD512	
707	BLH769		775	BXD435		843	BXD508	
708	BXD414		776	BXD433		844	BXD498	
709	BLH775		777	BXD430		845	BXD580	
710	BLH772		778	BXD452		846	BXD506	
711	BLH773		779	BXD438		847	BXD516	
712	BLH784		780	BXD461		848	BXD519	
713	BLH776		781	BXD439		849	BXD611	
714	BLH777		782	BXD440	21.8.44 b	850	BXD520	
715	BLH774		783	BXD446		851	BXD514	
716	BLH782		784	BXD429		852	BXD581	
717	BLH785		785	BXD428		853	BXD592	
718	BLH786		786	BXD457		854	BXD513	
719	BLH778		787	BXD456		855	BXD591	
720	BLH779		788	BXD448		856	BXD583	
721	BLH790		789	BXD450		857	BXD582	
722	BLH795		790	BXD462		858	BXD517	
723	BLH796		791	BXD453		859	BXD595	
724	BLH780		792	BXD447		860	BXD598	
725	BLH787		793	BXD484		861	CGJ20	
726	BLH781		794	BXD468		862	BXD603	
727	BLH791		795	BXD460		863	BXD587	
728	BLH783		796	BXD458		864	BXD597	
729	BLH792		797	BXD454		865	CGJ11	
730	BLH788		798	BXD464		866	BXD590	
731	BLH789		799	BXD469		867	BXD577	
732	BXD408		800	BXD465		868	BXD594	
733	BLH794		801	BXD459		869	CGJ18	
734	BXD421		802	BXD476		870	CGJ13	
735	BXD404		803	BXD467		871	BXD578	
736	BLH797		804	BXD463		872	BXD586	
737	BLH793		805	BXD480		873	BXD584	
738	BXD402		806	BXD474		874	CGJ15	

b Destroyed by bombing   tt Fitted with tunnel body during the war

STL		Date out of stock	STL		Date out of stock	STL		Date out of stock
875	BXD593		943	CGJ64		1011	BLH870	
876	CGJ17		944	CGJ48		1012	BLH889	
877	CGJ37		945	CGJ39		1013	BLH871	
878	CGJ27		946	CGJ45		1014	BLH867	
879	BXD609		947	CGJ65		1015	BLH881	
880	CGJ32		948	CGJ40		1016	BLH884	
881	CGJ21		949	CGJ31		1017	BLH873	
882	BXD608		950	CGJ46		1018	BLH872	
883	BXD612		951	CGJ47		1019	BLH876	
884	BXD601		952	CGJ68		1020	BLH877	
885	CGJ26		953	CGJ70		1021	BLH893	
886	BXD600		954	CGJ72		1022	BXD526	
887	CGJ29		955	CGJ75		1023	BLH895	
888	CGJ23		956	CGJ66		1024	BLH878	
889	BXD588		957	CGJ71		1025	BLH879	
890	BXD589		958	CGJ73		1026	BLH874	
891	BXD605		959	BLH816		1027	BLH880	
892	BXD616		960	BLH817		1028	BLH892	
893	BXD602		961	BLH830		1029	BLH896	
894	BXD618		962	BLH834		1030	BLH894	
895	BXD613		963	BLH826		1031	BLH891	
896	BXD604		964	BLH827		1032	BLH885	
897	BXD620		965	BLH824		1033	BLH897	
898	BXD596		966	BLH831		1034	BLH875	
899	BXD617		967	BLH822		1035	BLH899	
900	BXD607		968	BLH835		1036	BLH882	
901	BXD621		969	BLH818		1037	BLH883	
902	CGJ43		970	BLH823		1038	BLH900	
903	BXD614		971	BLH828		1039	BLH886	
904	CGJ22		972	BLH819		1040	BLH887	
905	CGJ28		973	BLH820		1041	BLH898	
906	BXD606		974	BLH832		1042	BLH888	
907	CGJ30		975	BLH829		1043	BLH890	
908	CGJ44		976	BLH821		†1044	BPE221	
909	CGJ14		977	BLH825		†1045	BPF269	
910	BXD599		978	BLH833		†1046	BPF270	
911	CGJ34		979	BLH836		†1047	BPF288	
912	CGJ51		980	BLH849		†1048	BPF289	
913	BXD619		981	BLH837		†1049	BPF391	
914	CGJ19		982	BLH838		†1050	BPF397	
915	CGJ12		983	BLH839		†1051	BPF416	
916	CGJ36		984	BLH851		†1052	BPF417	
917	CGJ24		985	BLH840		†1053	BPF456	
918	BXD615		986	BLH859		†1054	BPF457	
919	CGJ33		987	BLH847		†1055	BPF458	
920	CGJ56		988	BLH842		1056	BXD503	
921	CGJ54		989	BLH843		1057	BXD504	
922	CGJ55		990	BLH860		1058	BXD501	
923	CGJ35		991	BLH850		1059	BXD502	
924	CGJ50		992	BLH844		1060	CLE37	
925	CGJ62		993	BLH845		1061	CGJ76	
926	CGJ42		994	BLH865		1062	CGJ138	
927	CGJ38		995	BLH853		1063	CGJ122	
928	CGJ59		996	BLH848		1064	CGJ78	
929	CGJ63		997	BLH855		1065	CGJ116	
930	CGJ67		998	BLH841		1066	CGJ84	
931	CGJ16		999	BLH852		1067	CGJ79	
932	CGJ69		1000	BLH846		1068	CGJ80	
933	CGJ25		1001	BLH854		1069	CGJ109	
934	CGJ52		1002	BLH856		1070	CGJ83	
935	CGJ74		1003	BLH857		1071	CGJ104	
936	CGJ60		1004	BLH862		1072	CGJ134	
937	CGJ57		1005	BLH863		1073	CGJ81	
938	CGJ49		1006	BLH869		1074	CGJ89	
939	CGJ61		1007	BLH861		1075	CGJ102	
940	CGJ53		1008	BLH864		1076	CGJ85	
941	CGJ58		1009	BLH868		1077	CGJ90	
942	CGJ41		1010	BLH866		1078	CGJ86	

† Lowbridge body

STL		Date out of stock	STL		Date out of stock	STL		Date out of stock
1079	CGJ128		1147	CGJ141		1215	CLE58	
1080	CGJ129		1148	CGJ154		1216	CLE72	
1081	CLE30		1149	CLE21		1217	BLY145	
1082	CGJ127		1150	CGJ144		1218	BXB845	
1083	CLE45		1151	CGJ142		1219	CLE81	
1084	CGJ101		1152	CGJ148		1220	BXH409	
1085	CGJ117		1153	CLE38		1221	BXA711	
1086	CGJ87		1154	CGJ149		1222	BLD98	
1087	CGJ112		1155	CGJ155		1223	CLE79	
1088	CGJ91		1156	CLE23		1224	BUL279	
1089	CGJ118		1157	CLE41		1225	CLE74	
1090	CGJ82		1158	CGJ156		1226	CLE76	
1091	CGJ143		1159	CLE43		1227	BLN618	
1092	CLE20		1160	CLE15		1228	BUC516	
1093	CGJ137		1161	CGJ151		1229	BUL48	
1094	CGJ130		1162	CGJ157		1230	CLE91	
1095	CGJ123		1163	CLE42		1231	BYM463	
1096	CGJ93		1164	CLE16		1232	CLE95	
1097	CGJ115		1165	CLE18		1233	CLE90	
1098	CGJ88		1166	CLE44		1234	BUL347	
1099	CGJ92		1167	CLE31		1235	BUW595	
1100	CGJ146		1168	CLE32		1236	BLO239	
1101	CGJ98		1169	CLE52		1237	BLC45	
1102	CGJ103		1170	CLE24		1238	BLN216	
1103	CGJ126		1171	CLE28		1239	CLE92	
1104	CGJ111		1172	CLE40		1240	BLC518	
1105	CGJ105		1173	CLE50		1241	CLE89	
1106	CGJ94		1174	CLE27		1242	BXX857	
1107	CGJ152		1175	CLE25		1243	BXN283	
1108	CGJ97		1176	CLE73		1244	BGF545	
1109	CGJ100		1177	CLE75		1245	BXH468	
1110	CLE35		1178	CLE60		1246	BGO161	
1111	CGJ99		1179	CLE84		1247	BXD992	
1112	CGJ108		1180	CLE67		1248	BYE312	
1113	CGJ107		1181	CLE88		1249	BLT355	
1114	CGJ96		1182	CLE93		1250	CLE96	
1115	CGJ106		1183	BXX973		1251	BXH467	
1116	CLE85		1184	CLE54		1252	BXA618	
1117	CGJ95		1185	CLE48		1253	BXD695	
1118	CGJ133		1186	BXD401		1254	BXL215	
1119	CGJ139		1187	CLE55		1255	BUV785	
1120	CGJ113		1188	CLE49		1256	BUW576	
1121	CGJ114		1189	CLE53		1257	BXA886	
1122	CGJ124		1190	CLE64		1258	BXH603	
1123	CGJ131		1191	CLE86		1259	BXF31	
1124	CLE17		1192	CLE80		1260	CLE33	
1125	CGJ150		1193	CLE61		1261	CLE39	
1126	CGJ120		1194	CLE94		1262	CLE34	
1127	CLE12		1195	CLE59		1263	CLE36	
1128	CGJ110		1196	CLE56		1264	BYL812	
1129	DGX216		1197	CLE62		1265	BXU721	
1130	CGJ125		1198	CLE68		1266	BXO55	
1131	CLE13		1199	CLE51		1267	BYH255	
1132	CLE29		1200	CLE47		1268	BXN540	
1133	CLE26		1201	CLE63		1269	BXN355	
1134	CGJ147		1202	CLE57		1270	CLX514	
1135	CGJ135		1203	CLE70		1271	BXU722	
1136	CGJ121		1204	CLE87		1272	BXU715	
1137	CLE11		1205	CLE82		1273	BXY318	
1138	CGJ140		1206	CLE83		1274	BXO54	
1139	CGJ153		1207	BUW575		1275	BXU752	
1140	CLE46		1208	CLE69		1276	BYH256	
1141	CGJ119		1209	CLE78		1277	BYH912	
1142	CLE22		1210	CLE71		1278	BYK791	
1143	CGJ132		1211	BUW785		1279	BYH679	
1144	CGJ136		1212	CLE65		1280	BXW307	
1145	CGJ145		1213	CLE66		1281	BYE589	
1146	CLE14		1214	CLE77		1282	BXU800	

STL		Date out of stock	STL		Date out of stock	STL		Date out of stock
1283	BYH254		1351	CLX593		1419	CXX137	
1284	BXV161		1352	CLX539		1420	CXX208	
1285	BYF360		1353	CLX540		1421	CXX145	
1286	BXW136		1354	CLX579		1422	CXX138	
1287	BYM557		1355	CLX534		1423	CXX146	
1288	BYL960		1356	CLX581		1424	CXX136	
1289	CLX515		1357	CLX537		1425	CXX149	
1290	BYM556		1358	CXX111		1426	CXX142	
1291	BYM554		1359	CLX595		1427	CXX148	
1292	BYN974		1360	CLX583		1428	CXX176	
1293	BYN760		1361	CLX578		1429	CXX181	
1294	BYO913		1362	CLX535		1430	CXX150	
1295	BYN920		1363	CLX586		1431	CXX184	
1296	BYX961		1364	CLX592		1432	CXX201	
1297	BYR802		1365	CLX589		1433	CXX177	
1298	BYP4		1366	CLX584		1434	CXX187	
1299	BYP480		1367	CLX541		1435	CXX182	
1300	BYP481		1368	CLX538		1436	CXX178	
1301	BYO986		1369	CLX576		1437	CXX180	
1302	BYU319		1370	CXX130		1438	CXX186	
1303	BYU167		1371	CLX585		1439	CXX185	
1304	BYU385		1372	CXX106		1440	CXX183	
1305	BYT696		1373	CXX104		1441	CXX188	
1306	BYU164		1374	CLX597		1442	CXX189	
1307	CGC197		1375	CXX109		1443	CXX192	
1308	BYU392		1376	CLX590		1444	CXX196	
1309	BYU844		1377	CLX596		1445	CXX191	
1310	BYU845		1378	CXX114		1446	CXX190	
1311	CLF503		1379	CXX107		1447	CXX193	
1312	BYV557		1380	CXX125		1448	CXX194	
1313	BYY701		1381	CXX108		1449	CXX195	
1314	BYY835		1382	CLX594		1450	CXX205	
1315	CGU762		1383	CLX588		1451	CXX206	
1316	CGO129		1384	CXX139		1452	CXX197	
1317	BYX39		1385	CXX101		1453	CXX202	
1318	BYX979		1386	CXX102	6.12.40 b	1454	CXX207	
1319	CGF536		1387	CXX118		1455	CXX209	
1320	CGF540		1388	CXX115		1456	CXX203	
1321	CLO39		1389	CXX103		1457	CXX210	
1322	CLX511		1390	CXX116		1458	CXX199	
1323	CLX512		1391	CXX113		1459	CXX198	
1324	CLX516		1392	CXX110		1460	CXX200	
1325	CLX513		1393	CXX112		1461	CXX211	
1326	CLX530		1394	CXX120		1462	CXX204	
1327	CLX522		1395	CXX119		1463	CXX212	
1328	CLX517		1396	CXX105		1464	CXX451	
1329	CLX518		1397	CXX124		1465	CXX452	
1330	CLX519		1398	CXX122		1466	CXX453	
1331	CLX526		1399	CXX127		1467	CXX454	
1332	CLX523		1400	CXX126		1468	CXX455	
1333	CLX520		1401	CXX117		1469	CXX456	
1334	CXX143		1402	CXX121		1470	CXX457	
1335	CLX521		1403	CXX254		1471	CXX458	
1336	CLX524		1404	CXX128		1472	CXX459	
1337	CLX527		1405	CXX129		1473	CXX460	
1338	CLX525		1406	CXX123		1474	CXX461	
1339	CLX528		1407	CXX133		1475	CXX462	
1340	CLX577		1408	CXX131		1476	CXX463	
1341	CLX529		1409	CXX132		1477	CXX464	
1342	CLX531		1410	CXX134		1478	CXX465	
1343	CLX591		1411	CXX135		1479	CXX466	
1344	CLX532		1412	CXX141		1480	CXX467	
1345	CLX542		1413	CLE209		1481	CXX468	
1346	CLX533		1414	CLE210		1482	CXX469	
1347	CLX587		1415	CXX140		1483	CXX470	
1348	CLX582		1416	CXX147		1484	CXX471	
1349	CLX580		1417	CXX179		1485	CXX472	
1350	CLX536		1418	CXX144		1486	CXX473	

b Destroyed by bombing

STL		Date out of stock	STL		Date out of stock	STL		Date out of stock
1487	CXX474		1555	CXX261		1623	CXX334	
1488	CXX475		1556	CXX262		1624	CXX341	
1489	CXX476		1557	CXX263		1625	CXX330	
1490	CXX477		1558	CXX264		1626	CXX338	
1491	CXX478		1559	CXX280		1627	CXX337	
1492	CXX479		1560	CXX274		1628	CXX339	
1493	CXX480		1561	CXX268		1629	CXX336	
1494	CXX481		1562	CXX284		1630	CXX340	
1495	CXX482		1563	CXX267		1631	CXX351	
1496	CXX483		1564	CXX269		1632	CXX342	
1497	CXX484		1565	CXX279		1633	CXX361	
1498	CXX485		1566	CXX275		1634	CXX343	
1499	CXX486		1567	CXX276		1635	CXX344	
1500	CXX487		1568	CXX277		1636	CXX352	
1501	CXX488		1569	CXX278		1637	CXX374	
1502	CXX489		1570	CXX306		1638	CXX345	
1503	CXX490		1571	CXX298		1639	CXX346	
1504	CXX491		1572	CXX285		1640	CXX359	
1505	CXX492		1573	CXX281		1641	CXX347	
1506	CXX493		1574	CXX290		1642	CXX366	
1507	CXX494		1575	CXX282		1643	CXX348	
1508	CXX495		1576	CXX293		1644	CXX349	
1509	CXX496		1577	CXX283		1645	CXX365	
1510	CXX497		1578	CXX287		1646	CLE19	
1511	CXX498		1579	CXX299		1647	CXX363	
1512	CXX499		1580	CXX286		1648	CXX372	
1513	CXX500		1581	CXX292		1649	CXX360	
1514	CXX225		1582	CXX302		1650	CXX356	
1515	CXX218		1583	CXX291		1651	CXX350	
1516	CXX217		1584	CXX307		1652	CXX358	
1517	CXX213		1585	CXX304		1653	CXX355	
1518	CXX216		1586	CXX322		1654	CXX368	
1519	CXX226		1587	CXX288		1655	CXX362	
1520	CXX219		1588	CXX294		1656	CXX354	
1521	CXX221		1589	CXX303		1657	CXX367	
1522	CXX214		1590	CXX295		1658	DGX196	
1523	CXX215		1591	CXX300		1659	CXX357	
1524	CXX224		1592	CXX296		1660	DGX197	
1525	CXX227		1593	CXX301		1661	CXX369	
1526	CXX223		1594	CXX289		1662	CXX364	
1527	CXX220		1595	CXX308		1663	DLU172	
1528	CXX222		1596	CXX309		1664	CXX353	
1529	CXX235		1597	CXX325		1665	DGX198	
1530	CXX230		1598	CXX323		1666	CXX373	
1531	CXX234		1599	CXX321		1667	DGX213	
1532	CXX238		1600	CXX320		1668	CXX371	
1533	CXX239		1601	CXX297		1669	DGX199	
1534	CXX232		1602	CXX310		1670	CXX370	
1535	CXX228		1603	ELP293		1671	DGX200	
1536	CXX237		1604	CXX328		1672	DGX201	
1537	CXX242		1605	CXX315		1673	DGX202	
1538	CXX229		1606	CXX333		1674	DGX203	
1539	CXX233		1607	CXX311		1675	DGX204	
1540	CXX231		1608	CXX312		1676	DGX207	
1541	CXX240		1609	CXX314		1677	DGX205	
1542	CXX236		1610	CXX313		1678	DGX206	
1543	CXX241		1611	CXX316		1679	DGX210	
1544	CXX251		1612	CXX305		1680	DGX209	
1545	CXX246		1613	CXX324		1681	DGX217	
1546	CXX247		1614	CXX332		1682	DGX208	
1547	CXX252		1615	CXX329		1683	DGX211	
1548	CXX253		1616	CXX326		1684	DGX212	
1549	CXX245		††1617	CXX318		1685	CXX375	
1550	CXX266		1618	CXX317		1686	DGX193	
1551	CXX255		1619	CXX319		1687	CXX376	
1552	CXX260		1620	CXX327		1688	DGX254	
1553	CXX265		1621	CXX335		1689	CXX377	
1554	CXX259		1622	CXX331		1690	CXX379	

†† Mounted with lowbridge body, 1942–43

STL		Date out of stock	STL		Date out of stock	STL		Date out of stock
1691	CXX378		1759	DGX302		t 1827	DLU206	
1692	DGX191		1760	DGX303		t 1828	DLU207	
1693	DGX192		1761	DGX304		1829	DLU210	
1694	DGX214		1762	DGX305		t 1830	DLU196	
1695	CXX381		1763	DGX306		1831	DLU208	
1696	DGX215		1764	DGX307		1832	DLU198	
1697	CXX380		1765	DGX308		1833	DLU199	
1698	DGX218		1766	DGX309		1834	DLU200	
1699	DGX194		1767	DGX310		t 1835	DLU201	
1700	DGX219		1768	DGX311		1836	DLU202	
1701	DGX250		1769	DGX312		1837	DLU203	
1702	DGX195		1770	DGX313		1838	DLU204	
1703	DGX245		1771	DGX314		1839	DLU50	
1704	DGX246		1772	DGX315		1840	DLU192	
1705	DGX247		1773	DGX316		t 1841	DLU209	
1706	DGX248		1774	DGX317		t 1842	DLU242	
1707	DGX251		1775	DGX325		t 1843	DLU216	
1708	DGX252		1776	DGX330		t 1844	DLU213	
1709	DGX249		1777	DGX326		t 1845	DLU211	
1710	DGX255		1778	DGX331		t 1846	DLU212	
1711	DGX256		1779	DGX332		1847	DLU214	
1712	DGX265		1780	DGX333		t 1848	DLU218	
1713	DGX257		1781	DGX338		t 1849	DLU215	
1714	DGX261		1782	DGX339		t 1850	DLU219	
1715	DGX294		1783	DGX342		t 1851	DLU217	
1716	DGX262		1784	DGX340		t 1852	DLU224	
1717	DGX323		1785	DGX349		t 1853	DLU225	
1718	DGX258		1786	DGX341		t 1854	DLU221	
1719	DGX263		1787	DGX345		t 1855	DLU232	
1720	DGX264		1788	DGX346		t 1856	DLU222	
1721	DGX275		1789	DGX350		t 1857	DLU227	
1722	DGX259		1790	DGX359		t 1858	DLU226	
1723	DGX266		1791	DGX358		1859	DLU220	
1724	DGX267		1792	DGX356		t 1860	DLU228	
1725	DGX268		1793	DLU11		t 1861	DLU229	
1726	DGX269		1794	DLU14		t 1862	DLU223	
1727	DGX270		1795	DLU16		1863	DLU239	
1728	DGX271		1796	DGX360		t 1864	DLU236	
1729	DGX272		1797	DLU13		t 1865	DLU230	
1730	DGX273		1798	DLU20		t 1866	DLU237	
1731	DGX276		1799	DGX357		t 1867	DLU235	
1732	DGX277		1800	DLU15		t 1868	DLU233	
1733	DGX278		1801	DLU32		1869	DLU252	
1734	DGX279		1802	DLU29		1870	DLU231	
1735	DGX280		1803	DLU21		t 1871	DLU240	
1736	DGX283		1804	DLU17		t 1872	DLU238	
1737	DGX274		1805	DLU33		1873	DLU268	
1738	DGX324		1806	DLU30		t 1874	DLU241	
1739	DLU40		1807	DLU22		t 1875	DLU234	
1740	DLU292		1808	DLU34		t 1876	DLU243	
1741	DGX281		t 1809	DLU48		1877	DLU246	
1742	DGX284		1810	DLU36		1878	DLU289	
1743	DGX282		1811	DLU31		1879	DLU284	
1744	DGX286		1812	DLU41		1880	DLU248	
1745	DGX287		1813	DLU35		1881	DLU247	
1746	DGX285		t 1814	DLU188		1882	DLU259	
1747	DGX288		1815	DLU44		1883	DLU288	
1748	DGX289		1816	DLU42		t 1884	DLU244	
1749	DGX290		1817	DLU193		1885	DLU267	
1750	DGX291		t 1818	DLU189		1886	DLU253	
1751	DGX292		1819	DLU195		1887	DLU245	
1752	DGX293		1820	DLU194		1888	DLU280	
1753	DGX298		1821	DLU49		1889	DLU266	
1754	DGX295		1822	DLU45		1890	DLU251	
1755	DGX296		t 1823	DLU190		1891	DLU277	
1756	DGX297		1824	DLU205		1892	DLU249	
1757	DGX299		t 1825	DLU191		1893	DLU285	
1758	DGX301		1826	DLU197		1894	DLU250	

†† Mounted with lowbridge body, 1942–43   t Tunnel body

STL		Date out of stock	STL		Date out of stock	STL		Date out of stock
1895	DLU272		1963	DLU154		2031	DGX334	
1896	DLU255		1964	DLU158		2032	DGX347	
1897	DLU273		1965	DLU170		2033	DGX352	
1898	DLU256		1966	DLU169		2034	DGX353	
1899	DLU254		1967	DLU156		2035	DGX348	
1900	DLU293		1968	DLU164		2036	DGX354	
1901	DLU278		1969	BXT431		2037	DGX355	
1902	DLU260		1970	DLU166		2038	DLU23	
1903	DLU261		1971	DLU165		2039	DLU18	
1904	DLU274		1972	DLU167		2040	DLU38	
1905	DLU258		††1973	DLU171		2041	DLU24	
1906	DLU296		††1974	DLU168		2042	DLU25	
1907	DLU263		1975	BXU697		2043	DLU39	
1908	DLU275		1976	BYR792		2044	DLU19	
1909	DLU264		1977	BUW565		2045	DLU37	
1910	DLU279		††1978	BXW938		2046	DLU26	26.8.44 b
1911	DLU270		1979	CGK320		2047	DLU43	
1912	DLU265		1980	CGW270		2048	DLU27	
1913	DLU257		1981	CLT303		2049	DLU28	
1914	DLU262		1982	BYY149		2050	DLU46	
1915	DLU294		1983	CGU628		2051	DLU47	
1916	DLU308		1984	BYX384		2052	DLU53	
1917	DLU298		1985	CGF772		2053	DLU54	
1918	DLU276		1986	CGK953		2054	DLU51	
1919	DLU290		1987	CLN408		2055	DLU52	
1920	DLU269		1988	CGX49		2056	DLU55	
1921	DLU271		1989	CLM970		2057	DLU56	
1922	DLU300		††1990	CGU38		2058	DLU57	
1923	DLU281		1991	CGY212		2059	DLU58	
1924	DLU301		1992	CGW269		2060	DLU59	
1925	DLU152		1993	CGX48		2061	DLU60	
1926	DLU146		1994	CUV501		2062	DLU61	
1927	DLU286		1995	CLN413		2063	DLU62	
1928	DLU287		1996	CXU346		2064	DLU63	
1929	DLU282		1997	CGO914		2065	DLU64	
1930	DLU306		1998	CLN740		2066	DLU65	
1931	DLU302		1999	CGU222		2067	DLU66	
1932	DLU283		2000	CGY208		2068	DLU67	
1933	DLU291		2001	CLO846		2069	DLU68	
1934	DLU148		2002	CLW777		2070	DLU69	
1935	DLU140		2003	CGY607		2071	DLU70	
1936	DLU299		2004	CLO847		2072	DLU71	
1937	DLU145		2005	CLX700		2073	DLU72	
1938	DLU139		2006	DYL846		2074	DLU73	
1939	DLU141		2007	CGY428		2075	DLU74	
1940	DLU295		2008	CGY663		2076	DLU75	
1941	DLU304		2009	CLN401		2077	DLU76	
1942	DLU159		2010	CLU366		2078	DLU77	
1943	DLU142		2011	CLX21		2079	DLU78	
1944	DLU297		2012	CLW82		2080	DLU79	
1945	DLU303		2013	CLF885		2081	DLU80	
1946	DLU155		2014	DGX253		2082	DLU81	
1947	DLU143		2015	DGX300		2083	DLU82	
1948	DLU147		2016	DGX319		2084	DLU83	
1949	DLU307		2017	DGX320		2085	DLU84	
1950	DLU305		2018	DGX321		2086	DLU85	
1951	DLU138		2019	DGX318		2087	DLU86	
1952	DLU150		2020	DGX322		2088	DLU87	
1953	DLU151		2021	DGX327		2089	DLU88	
††1954	DLU144		2022	DGX335		2090	DLU89	
††1955	DLU149		2023	DGX328		2091	DLU90	
1956	DLU163		2024	DGX329		2092	DLU91	
1957	DLU153		2025	DGX337		2093	DLU92	
1958	CGP272		2026	DLU12		2094	DLU93	
††1959	DLU157		2027	DGX351		2095	DLU94	
1960	DLU161		2028	DGX343		2096	DLU95	
1961	DLU160		2029	DGX336		2097	DLU96	
1962	DLU162		2030	DGX344		2098	DLU97	

†† Mounted with lowbridge body, 1942–43   b Destroyed by bombing

STL		Date out of stock	STL		Date out of stock	STL		Date out of stock
2099	DLU98		2167	DYL819		2235	DYL859	
2100	DLU99		2168	DYL820		2236	DYL861	
2101	DLU100		2169	DYL821		2237	DYL910	
2102	DLU101		2170	DYL822		2238	DYL863	
2103	DLU102		2171	DYL823		2239	DYL911	
2104	DLU103		2172	DYL824		2240	DYL862	
2105	DLU104		2173	DYL825		2241	DYL864	
2106	DLU105		2174	DYL826		2242	DYL866	
††2107	DLU106		2175	DYL827		2243	DYL870	
2108	DLU107		2176	DYL828		2244	DYL869	
2109	DLU108		2177	DYL829		2245	DYL865	
2110	DLU109		2178	DYL830		2246	DYL871	
2111	DLU110		2179	DYL831		2247	DYL880	
2112	DLU111		2180	DYL832		2248	DYL868	
2113	DLU112		2181	DYL833		2249	DYL882	
2114	DLU113		2182	DYL834		††2250	DYL874	
2115	DLU114		2183	DYL835		2251	DYL875	
2116	DLU115		2184	DYL836		2252	DYL872	
2117	DLU116		2185	DYL837		2253	DYL876	
2118	DLU117		††2186	DYL838		2254	EGO331	
2119	DLU118		2187	DYL839		2255	DYL873	
2120	DLU119		2188	DYL840		2256	DYL887	
2121	DLU120		2189	CLF886		2257	DYL883	
2122	DLU121		2190	CLH881		2258	DYL888	
2123	DLU122		2191	CLL355		2259	DYL884	
2124	DLU123		2192	CLN407		2260	DYL877	
2125	DLU124		2193	CUU997		2261	DYL878	
2126	DLU125		2194	CXR252		2262	DYL881	
2127	DLU126		2195	CXL823		2263	DYL879	
2128	DLU127		2196	CXO566		2264	DYL886	
2129	DLU128		2197	CXR641		2265	DYL890	
2130	DLU129		2198	CLX652		2266	DYL889	
2131	DLU130		2199	CLR387		2267	DYL891	
2132	DLU131		2200	CXO903		2268	DYL892	
2133	DLU132		2201	CXR251		2269	DYL893	
2134	DLU133		2202	CXR254		2270	DYL894	
2135	DLU134		2203	CYL465		2271	EGO332	
2136	DLU135		2204	CYH783		2272	DYL898	
2137	DLU136		2205	CYT677		††2273	DYL901	
2138	DLU137		2206	CYF598		2274	EGO334	
2139	DYL791		2207	CYL841		2275	DYL899	
2140	DYL792		2208	CYT711		2276	DYL895	
2141	DYL793		2209	CYT710		2277	DYL902	
2142	DYL794		2210	CYR372		2278	DYL900	
2143	DYL795		2211	DYL841		2279	DYL903	
2144	DYL796		2212	CYU18		2280	DYL896	
2145	DYL797		2213	CYU76		2281	EGO333	
2146	DYL798		2214	CYU851		2282	EGO338	
2147	DYL799		2215	DYL849		2283	EGO335	
††2148	DYL800		2216	DYL850		2284	EGO336	
2149	DYL801		††2217	DYL843		2285	EGO339	
2150	DYL802		2218	DYL897		2286	EGO337	
2151	DYL803		2219	DYL842		2287	EGO342	
2152	DYL804		††2220	DYL853		2288	EGO349	
2153	DYL805		2221	DYL848		2289	EGO340	
2154	DYL806		2222	DYL845		2290	EGO341	
2155	DYL807		2223	DYL847		††2291	EGO354	
2156	DYL808		2224	DYL844		††2292	EGO343	
2157	DYL809		2225	DYL851		2293	EGO347	
2158	DYL810		2226	DYL854		2294	EGO350	
2159	DYL811		2227	DYL858		2295	EGO345	
2160	DYL812		2228	DYL852		2296	EGO348	
2161	DYL813		††2229	DYL855		2297	EGO370	
2162	DYL814		2230	DYL856		2298	EGO344	
2163	DYL815		2231	DYL857		2299	EGO352	
2164	DYL816		††2232	DYL860		2300	EGO363	
2165	DYL817		2233	DYL885		2301	EGO355	
2166	DYL818		2234	DYL867		2302	EGO356	

†† Mounted with lowbridge body, 1942–43

STL		Date out of stock	STL		Date out of stock	STL		Date out of stock
2303	EGO353		2371	EGO416		2439	ELP102	
2304	EGO351		2372	EGO439		2440	EGO486	
2305	EGO346		2373	EGO436		2441	ELP103	
2306	EGO364		2374	EGO412		2442	ELP104	
2307	EGO358		2375	EGO433		2443	EGO489	
2308	EGO376		2376	EGO425		2444	ELP114	
2309	EGO366		2377	EGO426		2445	ELP106	
2310	EGO371		2378	EGO417		2446	ELP109	
††2311	EGO367		2379	EGO418		2447	ELP107	
2312	EGO357		2380	EGO419		2448	ELP101	
2313	EGO420		2381	EGO451		2449	ELP105	
2314	EGO405		2382	EGO438		2450	ELP112	
2315	CLH173		2383	EGO440		2451	ELP111	
2316	EGO359		2384	EGO458		2452	ELP115	
2317	CLH861		2385	EGO431		2453	ELP110	
2318	EGO391		2386	EGO424		2454	ELP117	
2319	CLH885		2387	EGO432		2455	ELP118	
2320	EGO369		2388	EGO430		2456	ELP120	
2321	EGO365		2389	EGO427		2457	ELP119	
2322	EGO384		2390	EGO462		2458	ELP123	
2323	EGO379		2391	EGO445		2459	ELP113	
2324	EGO377		2392	EGO434		2460	ELP116	
2325	EGO368		2393	EGO441		2461	ELP121	
2326	EGO360		2394	EGO435		2462	ELP129	
2327	EGO402		2395	EGO437		2463	ELP124	
2328	EGO378		2396	EGO443		2464	ELP133	
2329	EGO361		2397	EGO448		2465	ELP126	
2330	EGO380		2398	EGO452		2466	ELP125	
2331	EGO399		2399	EGO442		2467	ELP138	
2332	EGO381		2400	EGO444		2468	ELP128	
2333	EGO372		2401	EGO477		2469	ELP122	
2334	EGO362		2402	EGO446		2470	ELP136	
2335	EGO398		2403	EGO456		2471	ELP127	
2336	EGO373		2404	EGO450		2472	ELP130	
2337	EGO382		2405	EGO453		2473	ELP131	
2338	EGO374		2406	EGO447		2474	ELP144	
2339	EGO383		2407	EGO457		2475	ELP132	
2340	EGO386		2408	EGO449		2476	ELP142	
2341	EGO394		2409	EGO454		2477	ELP154	
2342	EGO375		2410	EGO459		2478	ELP134	
2343	EGO385		2411	EGO473		2479	ELP135	
2344	EGO395		2412	EGO460		2480	ELP150	
2345	EGO422		2413	EGO455		2481	ELP143	
2346	EGO400		2414	EGO469		2482	ELP137	
2347	EGO390		2415	EGO466		2483	ELP139	
2348	EGO397		2416	EGO461		2484	ELP148	
2349	EGO387		2417	EGO470		2485	ELP147	
2350	EGO389		2418	EGO471	6.12.40 b	2486	ELP151	
2351	EGO396		2419	EGO467		2487	ELP141	
2352	EGO403		2420	EGO463		2488	ELP140	
2353	EGO388		2421	EGO474		2489	ELP146	
2354	EGO413		2422	EGO472		2490	ELP152	
2355	EGO401		2423	EGO475		2491	ELP145	
2356	EGO392		2424	EGO468	6.12.40 b	2492	ELP168	
2357	EGO393		2425	EGO480		2493	ELP156	
2358	EGO429		2426	EGO476		2494	ELP167	
2359	EGO404		2427	EGO478		2495	ELP162	
2360	EGO406		2428	EGO464		2496	ELP153	
2361	EGO407		2429	EGO479		2497	ELP165	
2362	EGO408		2430	EGO483		2498	ELP157	
2363	EGO414		2431	EGO465		2499	ELP164	
2364	EGO423		2432	EGO487		2500	ELP171	
2365	EGO409		2433	EGO481		2501	ELP163	
2366	EGO410		2434	EGO484		2502	ELP172	
2367	EGO421		2435	EGO488		2503	ELP158	
2368	EGO415		2436	EGO485		2504	ELP173	
2369	EGO428		tt 2437	ELP108		2505	ELP159	
2370	EGO411		2438	EGO482		2506	ELP169	

b Destroyed by bombing   †† Mounted with lowbridge body, 1942–43   tt Fitted with tunnel body during the war

STL

2507	ELP160
2508	ELP170
2509	ELP149
2510	ELP161
2511	ELP166
2512	ELP155
2513	ELP174
2514	ELP176
2515	ELP175
2516	FJJ676
2517	FJJ677
2518	FJJ678
2519	FJJ679
2520	FJJ680
2521	FJJ681
2522	FJJ682
2523	FJJ683
2524	FJJ684
2525	FJJ685
2526	FJJ686
2527	FJJ687
2528	FJJ688
2529	FJJ689
2530	FJJ690
2531	FJJ691
2532	FJJ692
2533	FJJ693
2534	FJJ694
2535	FJJ695
2536	FJJ696
2537	FJJ697
2538	FJJ698
2539	FJJ699
2540	FJJ700
2541	FJJ701
2542	FJJ702
2543	FJJ703
2544	FJJ704
2545	FJJ705
2546	FJJ706
2547	FJJ707
2548	FJJ708
2549	FJJ709
2550	FJJ710
2551	FJJ711
2552	FJJ712
2553	FJJ713
2554	FJJ714
2555	FJJ715
2556	FJJ716
2557	FJJ717
2558	FJJ718
2559	FJJ719
2560	FJJ720
2561	FJJ721
2562	FJJ722
2563	FJJ723
2564	FJJ724
2565	FJJ725

STL

2566	FJJ726
2567	FJJ727
2568	FJJ728
2569	FJJ729
2570	FJJ730
2571	FJJ731
2572	FJJ732
2573	FJJ733
2574	FJJ734
2575	FJJ735
2576	FJJ736
2577	FJJ737
2578	FJJ738
2579	FJJ739
2580	FJJ740
2581	FJJ741
2582	FJJ742
2583	FJJ743
2584	FJJ744
2585	FJJ745
2586	FJJ746
2587	FJJ747
2588	FJJ748
2589	FJJ749
2590	FJJ750
2591	FJJ751
2592	FJJ752
2593	FJJ753
2594	FJJ754
2595	FJJ755
2596	FJJ756
2597	FJJ757
2598	FJJ758
2599	FJJ759
2600	FJJ760
2601	FXT49
2602	FXT50
2603	FXT51
2604	FXT52
2605	FXT53
2606	FXT54
2607	FXT55
2608	FXT56
2609	FXT57
2610	FXT58
2611	FXT59
2612	FXT60
2613	FXT61
2614	FXT62
2615	FXT63
2616	FXT64
2617	FXT65
2618	FXT66
2619	FXT67
2620	FXT68
2621	FXT69
2622	FXT70
2623	FXT71
2624	FXT72

STL

2625	FXT73	
2626	FXT74	
2627	FXT75	
2628	FXT76	
2629	FXT77	
2630	FXT78	
2631	FXT79	
2632	FXT80	
2633	FXT81	
2634	FXT82	
2635	FXT83	
2636	FXT84	
2637	FXT85	
2638	FXT86	
2639	FXT87	
2640	FXT88	
2641	FXT89	
2642	FXT90	
2643	FXT91	
2644	FXT92	
2645	FXT93	
2646	FXT94	
2647	FXT95	
2648	FXT371	12.11.41
2649	FXT372	30.10.41
2650	FXT373	13.12.41
2651	FXT374	6.12.41
2652	FXT375	17.10.41
2653	FXT376	24.11.41
2654	FXT377	21.9.42
2655	FXT378	26.11.41
2656	FXT379	27.11.41
2657	FXT380	18.11.41
2658	FXT381	28.11.41
2659	FXT382	20.12.41
2660	FXT383	2.12.41
2661	FXT384	20.6.42
2662	FXT385	28.11.41
2663	FXT386	30.3.42
2664	FXT387	17.3.42
2665	FXT388	24.2.42
2666	FXT389	29.1.42
2667	FXT390	11.2.42
2668	FXT391	13.3.42
2669	FXT392	30.10.41
2670	FXT393	9.12.41
2671	FXT394	22.5.42
2672	FXT395	23.7.42
2673	FXT396	25.4.42
2674	FXT397	5.2.42
2675	FXT398	16.2.42
2676	FXT399	30.7.42
2677	FXT400	31.3.42
2678	FXT401	27.3.42
2679	FXT402	28.1.42
2680	FXT403	18.8.42
2681	FXT404	2.3.42

Q

Although the prototype and the 232 production vehicles were all single-deckers, there were five side-engined AEC 'Q' double-deckers (Q 2–5 and 188) of three types. Q 2 and 3 were fifty-six seaters built in 1934 by Metro-Cammell for Central Area service and therefore had a doorless entrance ahead of the front axle (2Q2). Q 4 and 5 were for Country Buses and had fifty-six seat centre entrance bodywork by Weymann (3Q3). All four had petrol engines, preselective gearboxes and fluid flywheels. The fifth double-decker (Q 188; 7Q7), built in 1937, was the only one to have an oil engine and was unique in having a three-axle chassis and air operated brakes. Its fifty-one seat centre-entrance Park Royal body was finished to Green Line specification as it was designed for operation on the busy Romford Green Line services, but its short working life was spent as a bus.

All the double-deckers were withdrawn from service in 1939 and put in store pending disposal but wartime restrictions on the sale of serviceable vehicles delayed their disposal. Q 3 was a bomb casualty at Swanley garage in 1941 and was scrapped but the other four were still in stock at the end of 1945.

Chassis:	AEC Q 762 (Q 2–5); AEC Q O763 (Q 188)
Engine:	AEC A167 7.4 litre 6-cylinder 110 bhp petrol (Q 2–5); A170 7.7 litre 6-cylinder 95 bhp oil (Q 188).
Transmission:	Daimler D129 4 speed preselective with fluid flywheel (Q 2,3); AEC D133 4 speed preselective with fluid flywheel (Q 4, 5, 188)
Bodywork:	Metro-Cammell (Q 2, 3); Weymann (Q 4, 5); Park Royal (Q 188)
Capacity:	H56F (Q 2, 3); H56CD (Q 4, 5); DPH51CD (Q 188)
	L.T. body and chassis codes:
	2Q2 (Q 2, 3); 3Q3 (Q 3, 4); 7Q7 (Q 188)
Built:	1934 (Q 2–5); 1937 (Q 188)
Number built:	5
Number in stock:	1. 1.40: 5 31.12.45: 4

Q		Date out of stock	Q		Q
2	AYV615		5	BPJ224	
3	AYV616	30.6.41	188	DGO500	
4	BPG507				

Lower deck view inside Q 188, in stock but out of use for the whole of the war.
London Transport

The metal-framed bodywork built by Leyland Motors Ltd for the STD class was the company's standard design, modified to resemble the Chiswick bodies on contemporary STLs. STD 92 was a 1STD1/1 because it was one of the ten fitted with torque convertors when they were new, although this had been replaced by a standard crash unit at its first overhaul. It is seen working from Hendon garage on route 113 at Oxford Circus stand.
Norman Anscombe collection

STD

In 1937, London Transport decided to accelerate the replacement of the obsolescent NS class and placed a then record order for 786 buses and coaches, of which 672 were double-deckers. As the Board was barred by statute from building more than 527 bodies a year, it was necessary to find alternative suppliers for some of the work. Leyland was chosen to share the body contract and the opportunity was taken to purchase complete buses so that an alternative source for chassis could also be tested. The one hundred Titans (STD 1–100) were nominally based on the standard TD4 and TD4c model Titan chassis but they were modified to meet London Transport's requirements, notably in having STL type low geared steering and revised dumb-irons so that the towing arrangements could be interchangeable with the STL. Ninety were fitted with crash gearboxes (STD 1–90) and ten with torque convertors (STD 91–100). The body-work was also the standard Leyland metal framed product modified in detail to resemble the latest style of roof-box STL. The torque converters were replaced by standard manual gearboxes at their first overhaul.

All one hundred pre-war STDs were originally allocated to Hendon garage where they supplied the entire vehicle requirement. Reductions in services following the outbreak of war in September 1939 threw up a surplus of STDs and these were allocated to Cricklewood garage in October 1939, for operation on route 16. In October 1942 the allocation was transferred from Cricklewood to Victoria, where they remained until the summer of 1945, after which they were again allocated exclusively to Hendon. Their transfer to Victoria followed the allocation to that garage of the unfrozen Titans, where STD 101 had entered service on route 22 on 1st December 1941.

STD 101–111 were part of London Transport's intake of non-standard vehicles during World War II. They were based on 'unfrozen' TD7 chassis, whose mechanical specification was broadly similar to the earlier Titans. The Park Royal bodywork was the first to be built to the Ministry of Supply's wartime austerity standard and STD 101 was the national prototype. As delivered only one single-piece indicator box was fitted, at the front, but London Transport fitted an additional display over the platform. A project to increase the number of opening windows to five on each side began in August 1945 and at about the same time a start was made on glazing the rear upper deck window. Earlier, in 1943, improvements had been made to the driving cab, including the provision of a quick-release emergency window and the replacement of plain by toughened glass.

The eleven unfrozen Titans which were added to the STD class in 1941/1942 were the first to be mounted with bodywork conforming to the Ministry of Supply's austerity specification. The Park Royal body on STD 111 was the national prototype and was built to the most rigid standards. Apparent in this official photograph are the reduced number of half-drop opening windows, the small destination blind aperture and the lack of curves. They were all allocated to Victoria garage and not to Camberwell as implied by the photograph and neither did they ever operate on night route 297. London Transport

The rear nearside view of STD 111 shows the unglazed rear emergency window, the angular 'dome' and the simple stop and tail-lights. To avoid the extra work involved in providing a recess for the registration plate, it has been placed on the rear saloon bulkhead, in a position similar to that used on the ST and LT classes. The bus has also been fitted with window netting with the first, unsuccessful, oblong type of passenger peephole. London Transport

Chassis:	Leyland Titan TD4 modified (STD 1–100); Leyland Titan TD7 (STD 101–111)		
Engine:	Leyland six cylinder 8.6 litre direct injection 94 bhp		
Transmission:	Leyland four speed crash (helical third speed)		
Bodywork	Leyland (STD 1–100); or Park Royal (STD 100–111)		
L. T. codes:	1STD1 (STD 1–90); 1STD1/1 (STD 91–100); 3STD2 (STD 101–111)		
Capacity:	H30/26R (STD 1–100); UH30/26R (STD 101–111)		
Built:	1937 (STD 1–100); 1941 (STD 101) 1942 (STD 102–111)		
Number built			
(by 31.12.45):	111		
Number in stock:	1.1.40: 100	31.12.45: 111	

STD   STD   STD

STD		STD		STD		Date into stock
1	DLU311	38	DLU348	75	DLU385	
2	DLU312	39	DLU349	76	DLU386	
3	DLU313	40	DLU350	77	DLU387	
4	DLU314	41	DLU351	78	DLU388	
5	DLU315	42	DLU352	79	DLU389	
6	DLU316	43	DLU353	80	DLU390	
7	DLU317	44	DLU354	81	DLU391	
8	DLU318	45	DLU355	82	DLU392	
9	DLU319	46	DLU356	83	DLU393	
10	DLU320	47	DLU357	84	DLU394	
11	DLU321	48	DLU358	85	DLU395	
12	DLU322	49	DLU359	86	DLU396	
13	DLU323	50	DLU360	87	DLU397	
14	DLU324	51	DLU361	88	DLU398	
15	DLU325	52	DLU362	89	DLU399	
16	DLU326	53	DLU363	90	DLU400	
17	DLU327	54	DLU364	91	DLU401	
18	DLU328	55	DLU365	92	DLU402	
19	DLU329	56	DLU366	93	DLU403	
20	DLU330	57	DLU367	94	DLU404	
21	DLU331	58	DLU368	95	DLU405	
22	DLU332	59	DLU369	96	DLU406	
23	DLU333	60	DLU370	97	DLU407	
24	DLU334	61	DLU371	98	DLU408	
25	DLU335	62	DLU372	99	DLU409	
26	DLU336	63	DLU373	100	DLU410	
27	DLU337	64	DLU374	101	FXT405	24.10.41
28	DLU338	65	DLU375	102	FXT428	12.3.42
29	DLU339	66	DLU376	103	FXT429	17.3.42
30	DLU340	67	DLU377	104	FXT430	18.5.42
31	DLU341	68	DLU378	105	FXT431	29.5.42
32	DLU342	69	DLU379	106	FXT432	22.5.42
33	DLU343	70	DLU380	107	FXT433	26.6.42
34	DLU344	71	DLU381	108	FXT434	6.7.42
35	DLU345	72	DLU382	109	FXT435	22.6.42
36	DLU346	73	DLU383	110	FXT436	30.7.42
37	DLU347	74	DLU384	111	FXT437	24.7.42

Announced as 'London's standard for years to come', the 2RT2s began to go into service in 1940, introducing the basic outline which was to become familiar to later generations as the standard London bus. At first, the RT2s did not have an offside headlamp, as can be seen in this view of RT 84 in June 1940. The curved driver's windscreen and cabside window were no doubt influenced by the 1930s fashion for streamlining and was to remain unique to the class. A.B. Cross

RT

The RT was a development of the AEC Regent chassis as used in the STL class but with an engine design strongly influenced by Leyland practice, following London Transport's successful operation of the one hundred 1937 Leyland Titans. At the end of the 1930s London Transport adopted a policy of having large engines, with a derated power output to improve fuel economy and engine life and the engine chosen for the RT was the AEC A185 9.6 litre unit, which developed 100 bhp at 1,800 rpm. The well tried Wilson type preselective gearbox and fluid flywheel were of the type used on the STL class but were actuated by compressed air, as were the brakes. Other features of the design were flexible engine mountings, improved and lighter steering, automatic chassis lubrication, automatic brake adjusters and a low bonnet and radiator. The prototype chassis first operated in service from Hanwell garage (HW) on route 18C between 13th July and 31st December 1938 with the number ST 1140 under a six year old fifty-six seat Dodson open staircase body originally carried by TD 111. A revolutionary new design of metal-framed body, with self-supporting rear platform, built at Chiswick Works, was then fitted and the vehicle numbered RT 1. The new body was of four bay construction and notable for its graceful curves, including the combined bulkhead and front wing assembly. Roof route number boxes were carried at both front and rear. RT 1 went into service on 9th August 1939.

Meanwhile an order had been placed for a production batch of 150, subsequently increased to 338 and the intention was to manufacture up to 527 a year from 1940 onwards. Following the outbreak of war on 3rd September 1939, government restrictions were placed on the construction of chassis for civilian use and the order for the last 188 was suspended. The 2RT2s (RT 2–151) differed from RT 1 in having composite bodywork for which the chassis frame was extended to support the platform in the conventional manner. Apart from this, only minor changes were made to tidy up the design. The mechanical specification was broadly the same, but the Bosch equipment and compressor for the air pressure system were replaced by components supplied by Clayton Dewandre. Five (RT 147–151) originally had experimental gearboxes with a smaller drum diameter.

Although often referred to incorrectly as 'pre-war' RTs, the 2RT2s were all built during the war, starting at the end of 1939. The first seven were licensed on 2nd January 1940, at Chelverton Road garage and operated on route 37. Later deliveries went to Putney Bridge and, after October 1941, Victoria. Soon after they went into service their air brake compressors began to give trouble, causing the brakes to operate erratically. As a precaution, deliveries to garages were stopped from mid-June 1940, by which time 108 were in service. All but twenty of those already in service were delicensed in July and August and placed in store to await modification to the bearings and seals. The twenty which remained licensed had either been modified already or were about to be. The modified vehicles began to return to service in September 1940 but it was not until December 1941 that the programme was completed. In the meantime, no new RTs had been licensed until March 1941, after which delivery of completed buses slowed down and the last twenty-four were spread over eleven months. The last did not go into service until 1st February 1942.

In their modified condition the compressors gave the necessary improvement to braking but had a very short life before there was risk of failure. A stronger compressor, of the reciprocating type instead of the rotary type fitted originally, was tried out towards the end of 1941 and found to be a considerable improvement. Fifty RTs were fitted with the new compressor but, because supplies were restricted, the programme was not completed until early in 1944. A further improvement tried out on RT 143 was for the drive to the air compressor to be by a belt from the engine instead of a shaft from the gearbox. This proved successful and, between March 1943 and August 1944, was applied to the same fifty RTs as had the new compressor. They were reclassified 1/2RT2/1.

After only three weeks in service in 1940, RT 19 was delicensed and returned to AEC who used it as a demonstrator between April 1940 and June 1942. It was painted in the light green and cream of Mansfield District Traction, which was the first operator, of at least twenty-two, to whom it was shown. Before it went on demonstration it was fitted with an engine with a toroidal combustion chamber, a specification close to that later adopted for the post-war model. In 1945 the chassis of RT 19 was remodelled as the prototype for the post-war version. This was similar to the 2RT but had a new engine, the A204, with toroidal cavity pistons and an increased power output of 125 bhp at 1,800 rpm (derated by LT to 115 bhp). The extension behind the rear axle was omitted as the platform on the new bodies was to be self-supporting. In November 1945 the body of RT 1, which had a self-supporting rear platform, was mounted on RT 19's modified chassis.

The RT class suffered no total losses as a result of enemy action but the body of RT 66 was damaged beyond repair by a flying bomb at the end of June 1944 and scrapped on 20th July. It was given the original body from RT 87, which had been repaired after bomb damage, in a series of body exchanges which included the transfer of RT 19's original body to RT 52. The renovated body now mounted on RT 66 was unique in having an offside route number plate holder set in the middle of the staircase panel. RT 97 was also badly damaged and was rebuilt for operation as a Pay-as-you-Board bus. It had yet to enter service as such at the end of 1945. One minor effect of war damage was the loss from RT 110 of its front roof route number box. All 151 2RT2s were still in stock at the end of 1945 but RT 1 was a bare chassis, RT 19 was in the process of being modified and RT 97 was standing by for service at Kingston in January 1946.

A rear view of RT 132 parked off-peak on Albert Embankment, showing full use of all the rear blind boxes, which proved short lived, and the white strips and disc to aid visibility during 'blackout' hours. W.J. Haynes

Chassis: AEC Regent III 0661
Engine: AEC A185 6-cylinder direct-injection 9.6 litre 100 bhp oil
Transmission: AEC D140 4-speed air operated preselective with fluid flywheel
Bodywork: LPTB (Chiswick)
Capacity: H30/26R (RT 1 H29/26R)
L.T. code: 1RT1 – later 1/2RT1 (RT 1); 2RT2 (RT 2–151)
Built: 1938/1939 (RT 1); 1939–1942 (RT 2–151)
Number built: 151 (by 31.12.45)
Number in stock: 1.1.40: 11   31.12.45: 151

RT		Date into stock	RT		Date into stock	RT		Date into stock
1	EYK396		52	FXT227	12.1.40	103	FXT278	11.4.40
2	FXT177	29.1.40	53	FXT228	12.1.40	104	FXT279	23.4.40
3	FXT178	18.1.40	54	FXT229	12.1.40	105	FXT280	9.4.40
4	FXT179	27.1.40	55	FXT230	11.4.40	106	FXT281	30.5.40
5	FXT180	1.1.40	56	FXT231	1.1.40	107	FXT282	4.4.40
6	FXT181	20.1.40	57	FXT232	12.1.40	108	FXT283	6.3.40
7	FXT182	6.2.40	58	FXT233	1.4.40	109	FXT284	1.4.40
8	FXT183	25.2.40	59	FXT234	17.1.40	110	FXT285	28.2.40
9	FXT184	6.2.40	60	FXT235	22.1.40	111	FXT286	6.6.40
10	FXT185	24.2.40	61	FXT236	24.1.40	112	FXT287	28.3.40
11	FXT186	13.3.40	62	FXT237	3.4.40	113	FXT288	7.3.40
12	FXT187	6.2.40	63	FXT238	25.1.40	114	FXT289	11.6.40
13	FXT188	21.2.40	64	FXT239	29.2.40	115	FXT290	7.3.40
14	FXT189	24.2.40	65	FXT240	12.4.40	116	FXT291	29.4.40
15	FXT190		66	FXT241	6.2.40	117	FXT292	10.4.40
16	FXT191		67	FXT242	28.2.40	118	FXT293	21.5.40
17	FXT192	4.3.40	68	FXT243	12.2.40	119	FXT294	26.4.40
18	FXT193	29.1.40	69	FXT244	30.5.40	120	FXT295	20.6.40
19	FXT194		70	FXT245	15.5.40	121	FXT296	27.4.40
20	FXT195		71	FXT246	4.6.40	122	FXT297	22.4.40
21	FXT196	16.2.40	72	FXT247	13.2.40	123	FXT298	10.6.40
22	FXT197	25.1.40	73	FXT248	8.3.40	124	FXT299	18.4.40
23	FXT198	29.1.40	74	FXT249	18.3.40	125	FXT300	3.5.40
24	FXT199	12.2.40	75	FXT250	25.5.40	126	FXT301	6.5.40
25	FXT200	1.1.40	76	FXT251	29.5.40	127	FXT302	5.4.40
26	FXT201	12.2.40	77	FXT252	15.4.40	128	FXT303	10.5.40
27	FXT202	22.1.40	78	FXT253	16.4.40	129	FXT304	1.5.40
28	FXT203	12.1.40	79	FXT254	15.3.40	130	FXT305	12.6.40
29	FXT204	18.1.40	80	FXT255	28.5.40	131	FXT306	7.5.40
30	FXT205	1.1.40	81	FXT256	16.4.40	132	FXT307	8.6.40
31	FXT206	12.1.40	82	FXT257	16.5.40	133	FXT308	17.4.40
32	FXT207	24.1.40	83	FXT258	19.4.40	134	FXT309	17.6.40
33	FXT208	21.3.40	84	FXT259	6.3.40	135	FXT310	24.6.40
34	FXT209	16.2.40	85	FXT260	6.4.40	136	FXT311	4.4.40
35	FXT210	17.1.40	86	FXT261	22.4.40	137	FXT312	11.5.40
36	FXT211	19.2.40	87	FXT262	27.3.40	138	FXT313	22.5.40
37	FXT212		88	FXT263	2.5.40	139	FXT314	22.4.40
38	FXT213		89	FXT264	6.8.40	140	FXT315	14.6.40
39	FXT214		90	FXT265	15.3.40	141	FXT316	24.5.40
40	FXT215	12.1.40	91	FXT266	31.5.40	142	FXT317	26.6.40
41	FXT216	20.1.40	92	FXT267	30.4.40	143	FXT318	17.6.40
42	FXT217	18.1.40	93	FXT268	14.5.40	144	FXT319	18.6.40
43	FXT218		94	FXT269	25.2.40	145	FXT320	13.6.40
44	FXT219		95	FXT270	2.4.40	146	FXT321	21.6.40
45	FXT220	29.3.40	96	FXT271	19.3.40	147	FXT322	1.3.41
46	FXT221	8.2.40	97	FXT272	29.4.40	148	FXT323	16.10.41
47	FXT222		98	FXT273	11.3.40	149	FXT324	18.8.41
48	FXT223	12.1.40	99	FXT274	19.2.40	150	FXT325	27.5.41
49	FXT224	1.1.40	100	FXT275	28.6.40	151	FXT326	14.1.42
50	FXT225	19.3.40	101	FXT276	3.6.40			
51	FXT226	10.2.40	102	FXT277	26.3.40			

The same style of Park Royal body as used on the STDs was supplied for the unfrozen Bristols which formed the new B class in 1942. B 5, at Greenford, reveals its pedigree as a standard pre-war K5G in its high set bonnet and radiator. S.L. Poole

B

B 1–9 comprised the third group of 'unfrozen' vehicles allocated to London Transport by the Ministry of War Transport and, like the STDs, had bodywork to austerity specification by Park Royal. The chassis were standard pre-war specification Bristol K5Gs, whose Gardner 5LW engines were the first to be purchased by London Transport. They were originally to be classified STB and the first two were shown in official records as STB 1 and 2. They may have been delivered with these numbers but when they entered service they were Bs. From 1943 onwards, the bodywork of the 1B1s was modified in the same way as the STDs.

Bristol was authorised to resume PSV production in 1945, using engines supplied by AEC, and twenty of the new K6A model were allocated to the Board (B 10–29). The second batch had Duple bodywork built to a 'relaxed austerity' specification, with five half-drop opening windows on each side, a side indicator box, glass in the rear emergency window, a rounded rear dome and moquette covered steel tubular-framed seats.

The first four 1B1s were licensed for service on 1st May 1942 and were allocated to Hanwell garage, where they operated on route 97. Hanwell operated the only Gardner-engined buses in the London Transport fleet at the time, the ten remaining 9LTs. The K6As were also allocated to Hanwell and the first two went into service on 12th December 1945. The remainder, although in stock, had yet to be licensed at the end of the year.

Relaxed austerity Duple bodywork was supplied for the twenty Bristol K6As delivered at the end of 1945. The combination of the simple but well proportioned lines of the body with the elegant newly introduced PV2 radiator, produced a satisfying result, despite the still austerity specification. *The Omnibus Society*

Chassis:	Bristol K5G (B 1–9); Bristol K6A (B 10–29)
Engine:AEC:	Gardner 5LW five-cylinder 7 litre 85 bhp oil (B 1–9);
	A202 7.7 litre direct injection 95 bhp oil (B 10–29)
Transmission:	Four speed crash.
Bodywork:	Park Royal (B 1–9); Duple (B 10–29)
Capacity:	UH30/26R
L.T. codes:	1B1 (B 1–9); 2B2 (B 10–29).
Built:	1942 (B 1–9); 1945 (B 10–29).
Number built:	29
Number in stock:	1.1.40: Nil; 31.12.45: 29

B		Date into stock	B		Date into stock	B		Date into stock
1	FXT419	26.3.42	11	HGC236	24.11.45	21	HGC246	10.12.45
2	FXT420	31.3.42	12	HGC237	27.11.45	22	HGC247	10.12.45
3	FXT421	9.4.42	13	HGC238	26.11.45	23	HGC248	13.12.45
4	FXT422	27.4.42	14	HGC239	28.11.45	24	HGC249	19.12.45
5	FXT423	22.4.42	15	HGC240	30.11.45	25	HGC250	17.12.45
6	FXT424	15.4.42	16	HGC241	3.12.45	26	HGC251	28.12.45
7	FXT425	6.5.42	17	HGC242	30.11.45	27	HGC252	29.12.45
8	FXT426	12.5.42	18	HGC243	6.12.45	28	HGC253	31.12.45
9	FXT427	30.4.42	19	HGC244	4.12.45	29	HGC254	22.12.45
10	HGC235	5.12.45	20	HGC245	7.12.45			

The first seventy-one London Guys had the original design of chassis, intended to be powered only by the Gardner 5LW engine, which enabled the radiator to be built more or less flush with the front dash. G 8 was a 2G2 with Park Royal bodywork of the same type as fitted to the STDs and Bs. Note the absence of anti-blast netting. The Omnibus Society

G

Once the supply of 'unfrozen' chassis had been exhausted in 1942, the Government authorised Guy Motors of Wolverhampton to build a limited number of new double-deck bus chassis to a strict austerity specification which required the use of substitute materials to economise on scarce resources such as aluminium alloys. This and the similar requirements for bodywork had the effect of increasing the unladen weight of the utilities by up to twenty per cent. The first five hundred chassis built by Guy were designed to be powered by the Gardner 5LW engine and London Transport was allocated eighty-four. Thirteen were later diverted to other operators, which reduced the number received to seventy-one. The specification was then changed to accommodate the 6LW engine, whose greater length required an extended bonnet which was fitted to all subsequent examples whichever engine was used. No 6LWs were allocated to London Transport. From G 72 onwards the Guys were 4½ inches longer than the permitted overall length of twenty-six feet, this breach being allowed by dispensation under Defence Regulations. This removed the need to shorten the body and there was no loss of passenger capacity. Between 1942 and 1945 London Transport was allocated a total of 435 Guy Arab chassis but no fewer than 297 were sanctioned during 1945 and, of these, all but two were delivered after the end of hostilities in Europe.

The standard gearbox on the wartime Guys was a sliding mesh crash unit but this was superseded in 1945 by a constant mesh version which was fitted to G 301–311 and 340–357. London Transport had already carried out an experiment with constant mesh gearboxes in October 1944 when the crash boxes on five Guys at Tottenham were replaced (G 7, 18, 19, 26 and 40). A later experiment in January 1945 involved the installation of synchromesh boxes on nine Arabs (G 3, 4, 8, 10, 14, 17, 20, 32 and 54), all allocated to Tottenham for comparison with crash and constant mesh versions.

Bodywork built before the middle of 1945 was also to strict austerity standards with no curves nor embellishments, no glazing in the rear upper deck emergency window, only two opening windows on each deck and only one single aperture indicator box. Early deliveries had leather covered spring cushioned seats but material shortages

Weymann became the second supplier of austerity bodywork to London in November 1942 when the first of a batch of eighteen 1/2G3s was delivered. Although the basic design closely resembled the Park Royal version, the Weymanns could be distinguished by their narrower ventilator apertures on the front upper deck windows, the absence of the slight bulge in the dash below the windscreen and the taller cab door and offside window. Until London Transport could produce an appropriate name plate of their own, the early Guys displayed the maker's name prominently, as can be seen on G 39 which was photographed at The Angel, Edmonton. The Omnibus Society

later imposed the use of wooden slatted seats on some vehicles; liveries also varied from standard red and white to various shades of brown with some being finished in overall grey. From G 137 onwards the specification was gradually relaxed to include rounded roof domes, more opening windows, improved seating and side indicator boxes. Gs 137 and 138 (Weymann) and 150 (Park Royal) were early prototypes for post-war production and had metal framed bodywork with a higher standard of finish.

Apart from one Duple body on G 43, Park Royal and Weymann were the main suppliers of bodywork until 1945 when first Massey, then Northern Counties were added, both with distinctively different designs, and finally Northern Coachbuilders who built twenty-six sub-contracted from Park Royal. Massey produced one of the most angular of the austerity designs, with no curves even on those bodies built under the relaxed specification. The Northern Counties version was metal-framed and had a smoother outline with a heavily curved rear upper deck almost giving it the appearance of a peacetime product. The Northern Coachbuilders' bodies were identical to the Park Royal product. The Park Royal body of G 30 was destroyed by bombing in July 1944 and replaced by a new austerity Northern Coach Builders body later that year.

G 1 was licensed at Tottenham garage on 1st December 1942 for service on route 76 where it was joined by five more by the end of the year, the first batch of forty-two being in stock by the end of January 1943. A number of design deficiencies had been discovered before the buses entered service and most had to go back to Guys for various modifications. More problems arose in service, including trouble with the brakes, and all but a handful were delicensed on 1st March 1943 so that modifications could be made, all returning to service by June. The only other garage to receive the Arab I version when new was Hanwell, where they ran on routes 18C (renumbered 92 in 1944) and 83/83A. A further six garages took delivery of Guys in the next three years, Alperton, Barking, Victoria, Upton Park, Hornchurch and Enfield. The allocation to Victoria in July 1945 was very unpopular with drivers and was quickly abandoned, the entire allocation of forty-five being transferred to Enfield in October. All but nineteen of the wartime Guy Arabs were in stock by the end of 1945.

The first Arab IIs again had bodywork by Park Royal, who were responsible for all but two of the new model delivered to London in 1943 and 1944. Although the body design did not change, their appearance was distinguished by the longer bonnet and the forward sweep of the mudguards. G 109, a 3G5, was one of a large batch allocated to route 18C (which became 92/92A in June 1944) and 83 from Hanwell, the second garage to receive the type, where they joined their Gardner-engined counterparts in the B class. J.F Higham Collection

After a lull of over a year, apart from the delivery of G 137 and 138, production of Guys for London resumed in April 1945 with the arrival of buses from a body manufacturer new to London Transport, Massey Brothers of Wigan, breaking the enviable degree of standardisation so far achieved. Most of these vehicles went into service after the end of the war in Europe and did not have blackout trim but, as this view of G 183 at Royal Forest Hotel Chingford shows, they were uncompromisingly austere in appearance. The Massey Guys, classified 1/3G9, were finished in two shades of brown, with no relief colour, but the relaxed Ministry of Supply specification now permitted additional opening windows and a glazed rear emergency window. S.L. Poole

Bodies from another manufacturer new to London Transport, Northern Counties Motor Engineering Ltd, coincidentally also from Wigan, began to arrive at the beginning of May 1945. Unusually for wartime bodies, they had metal-framed construction and their elegant design and relaxed austerity specification resembled peace-time standards. Although these were also delivered in brown livery, they had a pleasingly contrasting cream band. G 239 was one of the later G10/1s which had nearside indicator displays but no front ventilators. It is seen on the south side of Lambeth Bridge in Albert Embankment during the short-lived allocation of the class to Victoria garage. R.H.G. Simpson

Chassis:	Guy Arab I (G 1–71); Arab II (G 72–430)
Engine: Gardner:	5LW five-cylinder 7 litre 85 bhp oil
Transmission:	Four speed sliding mesh crash with double plate clutch (G 1–300, 312–339, 358–430); speed constant mesh (G 301–311, 340–357)
Bodywork:	Park Royal (G 1–31*, 51–136, 150, 206–218, 319–357); N.C.B. (G 139–149, 151–153, 194–205); Weymann (G 32–42, 44–50, 137, 138, 369–430); Duple (G 43); Northern Counties (G 154–173, 219–257, 269–311); Massey (G 174–193, 258–268, 312–318, 358–368).
Capacity:	UH30/26R
L.T. chassis codes:	2G (G 1–10), 1/2G (G 11–71), 3G (G 72–138), 1/3G (G 139–149, 151-300, 312–339, 358–430), 2/3G (G 301–311, 340–349), 4/3G (G 150)
L.T. body codes:	G2 (G 1–31, 51–71), G3 (G 32–42, 44–50), G4 (G 43), G5 (G 72–136), G6 (G 137), G6/1 (G 138), G7 (G 30)*, G8 (G 139–149, 151–153, 194–205), G8/1 (G 206–218), G8/2 (G 319–357), G9 (G 174–193, 258–268, 312–318, 358–368), G10 (G 154–173), G10/1 (G 219–257, 269–307), G11 (G 369–430), G12 (G 150).
Built:	1942–1945
Number built:	416 (still being delivered)
Number in stock:	1.1.40: Nil; 31.12.45: 416

* G 30 was mounted with a Northern Coachbuilders body (classified G10) in 1944

G		Date into stock	G		Date into stock	G		Date into stock
1	GLF651	18.9.42	6	GLF656	20.10.42	11	GLF661	6.11.42
2	GLF652	29.9.42	7	GLF657	26.10.42	12	GLF662	4.11.42
3	GLF653	17.10.42	8	GLF658	28.10.42	13	GLF663	9.11.42
4	GLF654	17.10.42	9	GLF659	5.11.42	14	GLF664	13.11.42
5	GLF655	19.10.42	10	GLF660	5.11.42	15	GLF665	16.11.42

G		Date into stock	G		Date into stock	G		Date into stock
16	GLF666	20.11.42	86	GLL585	7.8.43	156	GYL295	7.5.45
17	GLF667	24.11.42	87	GLL586	14.8.43	157	GYL296	10.5.45
18	GLF668	1.12.42	88	GLL587	14.8.43	158	GYL297	15.5.45
19	GLF669	26.11.42	89	GLL588	18.8.43	159	GYL298	10.5.45
20	GLF670	27.11.42	90	GLL589	20.8.43	160	GYL299	15.5.45
21	GLF671	28.11.42	91	GLL590	26.8.43	161	GYL300	24.5.45
22	GLF672	4.12.42	92	GLL591	20.8.43	162	GYL301	24.5.45
23	GLF673	7.12.42	93	GLL592	7.9.43	163	GYL302	31.5.45
24	GLF674	9.12.42	94	GLL593	8.9.43	164	GYL303	29.5.45
25	GLF675	12.12.42	95	GLL594	9.9.43	165	GYL304	28.5.45
26	GLF676	11.12.42	96	GLL595	11.9.43	166	GYL305	28.5.45
27	GLF677	15.12.42	97	GLL596	16.10.43	167	GYL306	4.6.45
28	GLF678	17.12.42	98	GLL597	20.10.43	168	GYL307	29.5.45
29	GLF679	21.12.42	99	GLL598	22.10.43	169	GYL308	31.5.45
30	GLF680	22.12.42	100	GLL599	8.11.43	170	GYL309	6.6.45
31	GLF681	23.12.42	101	GXE541	18.12.43	171	GYL310	4.6.45
32	GLF682	18.11.42	102	GXE542	23.12.43	172	GYL311	6.6.45
33	GLF683	20.11.42	103	GXE543	23.12.43	173	GYL312	8.6.45
34	GLF684	27.11.42	104	GXE544	23.12.43	174	GYL313	18.4.45
35	GLF685	27.11.42	105	GXE545	24.12.43	175	GYL314	18.4.45
36	GLF686	5.12.42	106	GXE546	24.12.43	176	GYL315	17.4.45
37	GLF687	5.12.42	107	GXE547	30.12.43	177	GYL316	20.4.45
38	GLF688	11.12.42	108	GXE548	30.12.43	178	GYL317	17.4.45
39	GLF689	21.12.42	109	GXE549	10.1.44	179	GYL318	25.4.45
40	GLF690	23.12.42	110	GXE550	31.12.43	180	GYL319	20.4.45
41	GLF691	1.1.43	111	GXE551	4.1.44	181	GYL320	24.4.45
42	GLF692	5.1.43	112	GXE552	5.1.44	182	GYL321	24.4.45
43	GLF693	25.1.43	113	GXE553	4.1.44	183	GYL322	1.5.45
44	GLF694	24.2.43	114	GXE554	5.1.44	184	GYL323	25.4.45
45	GLF695	10.3.43	115	GXE555	26.1.44	185	GYL324	27.4.45
46	GLF696	12.3.43	116	GXE556	26.1.44	186	GYL325	27.4.45
47	GLF697	23.3.43	117	GXE557	28.1.44	187	GYL326	2.5.45
48	GLF698	19.3.43	118	GXE558	27.1.44	188	GYL327	2.5.45
49	GLF699	20.4.43	119	GXE559	29.1.44	189	GYL328	14.5.45
50	GLF700	16.4.43	120	GXE560	1.2.44	190	GYL329	14.5.45
51	GLL551	11.2.43	121	GXE561	29.1.44	191	GYL330	17.5.45
52	GLL552	3.3.43	122	GXE562	3.2.44	192	GYL331	17.5.45
53	GLL553	6.3.43	123	GXE563	3.2.44	193	GYL332	23.5.45
54	GLL554	18.3.43	124	GXE564	3.2.44	194	GYL333	5.7.45
55	GLL555	20.3.43	125	GXE565	5.2.44	195	GYL334	5.7.45
56	GLL556	23.3.43	126	GXE566	5.2.44	196	GYL335	20.8.45
57	GLL557	27.3.43	127	GXE567	8.2.44	197	GYL336	23.8.45
58	GLL558	25.3.43	128	GXE568	9.2.44	198	GYL337	24.8.45
59	GLL559	31.3.43	129	GXE569	11.2.44	199	GYL338	23.8.45
60	GLL560	7.4.43	130	GXE570	15.2.44	200	GYL339	25.8.45
61	GLL561	14.4.43	131	GXE571	11.2.44	201	GYL340	25.8.45
62	GLL562	17.4.43	132	GXE572	12.2.44	202	GYL341	28.8.45
63	GLL563	10.4.43	133	GXE573	14.2.44	203	GYL342	29.8.45
64	GLL564	17.4.43	134	GXE574	15.2.44	204	GYL343	29.8.45
65	GLL565	22.4.43	135	GXE575	17.2.44	205	GYL344	31.8.45
66	GLL566	20.4.43	136	GXE576	22.2.44	206	GYL345	1.10.45
67	GLL567	3.5.43	137	GXV793	28.12.44	207	GYL346	19.9.45
68	GLL568	11.5.43	138	GXV794	28.3.45	208	GYL347	27.9.45
69	GLL569	8.5.43	139	GYE83	4.5.45	209	GYL348	21.9.45
70	GLL570	15.5.43	140	GYE84	1.6.45	210	GYL349	3.10.45
71	GLL571	15.5.43	141	GYE85	1.6.45	211	GYL350	2.10.45
72	GLL572	5.7.43	142	GYE86	2.6.45	212	GYL351	5.10.45
73	GLL573	1.7.43	143	GYE87	5.6.45	213	GYL352	16.10.45
74	GLL574	24.6.43	144	GYE88	5.6.45	214	GYL353	5.10.45
75	GLL575	22.6.43	145	GYE89	6.6.45	215	GYL354	6.10.45
76	GLL576	26.6.43	146	GYE90	7.6.45	216	GYL355	9.10.45
77	GLL577	30.6.43	147	GYE91	8.6.45	217	GYL356	10.10.45
78	GLL578	28.6.43	148	GYE92	9.6.45	218	GYL357	13.10.45
79	GLL579	9.7.43	149	GYE93	9.6.45	219	GYL358	12.6.45
80	GLL580	22.7.43	150	GYE94	1.9.45	220	GYL359	19.6.45
81	GLL581	24.7.43	151	GYE95	30.6.45	221	GYL360	19.6.45
82	GLL582	5.8.43	152	GYE96	30.6.45	222	GYL361	21.6.45
83	GLL583	13.9.43	153	GYE97	30.6.45	223	GYL362	20.6.45
84	GLL584	9.8.43	154	GYL293	1.5.45	224	GYL363	19.6.45
85	GLL600	9.8.43	155	GYL294	7.5.45	225	GYL364	20.6.45

G		Date into stock	G		Date into stock	G		Date into stock
226	GYL365	21.6.45	290	GYL430	30.10.45	368	HGC147	5.9.45
227	GYL366	23.6.45	291	GYL431	30.10.45	369	HGC148	31.8.45
228	GYL367	3.7.45	292	GYL432	18.10.45	370	HGC149	5.9.45
229	GYL368	23.6.45	293	GYL433	9.11.45	371	HGC150	17.9.45
230	GYL369	3.7.45	294	GYL434	12.11.45	372	HGC151	3.9.45
231	GYL370	3.7.45	295	GYL435	9.11.45	373	HGC152	5.9.45
232	GYL371	3.7.45	296	GYL436	12.11.45	374	HGC153	17.9.45
233	GYL372	3.7.45	297	GYL437	12.11.45	375	HGC154	10.9.45
234	GYL373	6.7.45	298	GYL438	23.11.45	376	HGC155	6.9.45
235	GYL374	6.7.45	299	GYL439	27.11.45	377	HGC156	17.9.45
236	GYL375	20.7.45	300	GYL440	23.11.45	378	HGC157	10.9.45
237	GYL376	6.7.45	301	GYL441	13.12.45	379	HGC158	18.9.45
238	GYL377	20.7.45	302	GYL442	13.12.45	380	HGC159	19.9.45
239	GYL378	23.7.45	303	GYL443	28.12.45	381	HGC160	18.9.45
240	GYL379	25.7.45	304	GYL444	13.12.45	382	HGC161	24.9.45
241	GYL380	27.7.45	305	GYL445	28.12.45	383	HGC162	19.9.45
242	GYL381	25.7.45	306	GYL446	28.12.45	384	HGC163	24.9.45
243	GYL382	27.7.45	312	GYL452	12.7.45	385	HGC164	26.9.45
244	GYL383	10.8.45	313	GYL453	25.7.45	386	HGC165	3.10.45
245	GYL384	21.8.45	314	GYL454	25.7.45	387	HGC166	24.9.45
246	GYL385	22.8.45	315	GYL455	30.7.45	388	HGC167	26.9.45
247	GYL386	22.8.45	316	GYL456	30.7.45	389	HGC168	28.9.45
248	GYL387	27.8.45	317	GYL457	30.7.45	390	HGC169	8.10.45
249	GYL388	29.8.45	318	GYL458	3.8.45	391	HGC170	27.9.45
250	GYL389	25.9.45	319	GYL459	17.11.45	392	HGC171	3.10.45
251	GYL390	27.9.45	320	GYL460	22.11.45	393	HGC172	8.10.45
252	GYL391	27.9.45	321	HGC100	17.11.45	394	HGC173	3.10.45
253	GYL392	30.10.45	322	HGC101	22.11.45	395	HGC174	3.10.45
254	GYL393	22.10.45	323	HGC102	21.11.45	396	HGC175	5.10.45
255	GYL394	8.11.45	324	HGC103	23.11.45	397	HGC176	10.10.45
256	GYL395	8.11.45	325	HGC104	23.11.45	398	HGC177	8.10.45
257	GYL396	8.11.45	326	HGC105	26.11.45	399	HGC178	12.10.45
258	GYL397	15.6.45	327	HGC106	27.11.45	400	HGC179	10.10.45
259	GYL398	15.6.45	328	HGC107	5.12.45	401	HGC180	15.10.45
260	GYL399	22.6.45	329	HGC108	4.12.45	402	HGC181	17.10.45
261	GYL400	22.6.45	330	HGC109	5.12.45	403	HGC182	17.10.45
262	GYL401	3.7.45	331	HGC110	29.11.45	404	HGC183	18.10.45
263	GYL402	3.7.45	332	HGC111	28.11.45	405	HGC184	15.10.45
264	GYL403	12.7.45	333	HGC112	26.11.45	406	HGC185	18.10.45
265	GYL404	12.7.45	334	HGC113	28.11.45	407	HGC186	18.10.45
266	GYL405	11.7.45	335	HGC114	1.12.45	408	HGC187	20.10.45
267	GYL406	7.7.45	336	HGC115	4.12.45	409	HGC188	24.10.45
268	GYL407	11.7.45	337	HGC116	3.12.45	410	HGC189	22.10.45
269	GYL409	3.8.45	338	HGC117	4.12.45	411	HGC190	26.10.45
270	GYL410	4.8.45	339	HGC118	10.12.45	412	HGC191	24.10.45
271	GYL411	10.8.45	340	HGC119	8.12.45	413	HGC192	24.10.45
272	GYL412	10.8.45	341	HGC120	13.12.45	414	HGC193	26.10.45
273	GYL413	21.8.45	342	HGC121	13.12.45	415	HGC194	31.10.45
274	GYL414	27.8.45	343	HGC122	15.12.45	416	HGC195	26.10.45
275	GYL415	29.8.45	344	HGC123	19.12.45	417	HGC196	31.10.45
276	GYL416	31.8.45	345	HGC124	20.12.45	418	HGC197	5.11.45
277	GYL417	31.8.45	346	HGC125	20.12.45	419	HGC198	31.10.45
278	GYL418	13.9.45	347	HGC126	28.12.45	420	HGC199	7.11.45
279	GYL419	25.9.45	348	HGC127	22.12.45	421	HGC200	5.11.45
280	GYL420	28.9.45	358	HGC137	7.8.45	422	HGC201	10.11.45
281	GYL421	8.10.45	359	HGC138	7.8.45	423	HGC202	7.11.45
282	GYL422	8.10.45	360	HGC139	13.8.45	424	HGC203	15.11.45
283	GYL423	8.10.45	361	HGC140	13.8.45	425	HGC204	10.11.45
284	GYL424	11.10.45	362	HGC141	13.8.45	426	HGC205	7.11.45
285	GYL425	11.10.45	363	HGC142	23.8.45	427	HGC206	14.11.45
286	GYL426	11.10.45	364	HGC143	23.8.45	428	HGC207	15.11.45
287	GYL427	18.10.45	365	HGC144	1.9.45	429	HGC208	14.11.45
288	GYL428	18.10.45	366	HGC145	5.9.45	430	HGC209	5.12.45
289	GYL429	22.10.45	367	HGC146	1.9.45			

Lower deck of a Duple bodied lowbridge D when new. The wooden slatted seats were more comfortable than they looked but gave a strongly austere appearance in common with the exterior though in contrast with the repp covered bulkhead. London Transport

D

Daimler was authorised by the Ministry of Supply to resume production of bus chassis at a temporary factory in Wolverhampton from the end of 1942. The first one hundred were powered by the Gardner 5LW engine and classified CWG5 but none of these was allotted to London. Surprisingly, the company was able to get authority to retain the pre-war Daimler specification of preselective gearbox and fluid transmission and the resulting vehicle was therefore the least austerity of the wartime models, although the use of cast iron instead of aluminium alloys was common to all. To fill the gap left when the supply of Gardner engines allocated to Daimler had been exhausted, AEC was authorised to resume production of its A173 7.7 litre engine, which became available during 1943. The new model was classified CWA6 and was very close in mechanical specification to the last batches of STL. Between October 1943 and June 1945, London Transport was granted seven separate allotments of Daimlers, totalling 181 chassis, of which 141 complete vehicles had been taken into stock by the end of 1945.

The first six (D 1–6) had lowbridge bodywork by Duple, for use on route 127 from Merton garage. The first chassis was delivered on 15th February 1944 and the first completed vehicle, D 1, arrived on 24th April. They went into service in April and May. A further four lowbridge examples (D 128–131) constituted the penultimate sanction, for which the bodywork contract had been assigned to Massey but this was transferred to Duple who supplied bodywork to the 'relaxed austerity' standard. These went into service at the end of 1945.

Bodywork for the highbridge utility Daimlers was supplied by both Brush (seventy-four) and Duple (forty-seven by the end of 1945, with a further forty to come). The first highbridge example, D 7, was received from Duple on 20th July 1944 and went into service on 2nd August. The first with Brush bodywork arrived on 26th January 1945. In contrast to the widespread allocation of the Guys, all Daimlers licensed before the end of 1945 were allocated to Merton garage.

The last vehicle in the final Brush-bodied batch, D 127, had a modified chassis, classified CWD6, incorporating the new Daimler 8.6 litre CD6 engine and also a new Daimler rear axle. Twelve of the final batch with Duple bodywork were also to be CWD6s, four having been delivered by the end of 1945.

Materials were in exceptionally short supply when the lowbridge Duple-bodied 1D1s were built and their full austerity specification was expanded to include wooden slatted seats. The problem did not extend to paint and they were finished in standard red and white with the between decks moulding picked out in black, a feature not to be found on any other utilities. As can be seen on D 4, photographed when still new, the anti-blast netting on these vehicles was applied only to the bottom half of the upper deck windows, whether fixed or half-drop, which was presumably a better way of allowing passengers to see out than through the diamond-shaped peephole which did not suit the higher position of the upstairs seats. The cabs on Duple utility bodies had a high waist line, which was slightly more exaggerated on the lowbridge version. No external advertisements were carried on the lowbridge Ds during the period under review, possibly because the moulding below the upper deck windows left too shallow a space. The Omnibus Society

The first batch of highbridge bodies on CWA6 chassis were also supplied by Duple to a design which was a clear derivative of the lowbridge type, the only external difference, apart from the height, being the continuous rain shields above the windows. As can be seen clearly in this photograph of D 8 taken at Acton Green, the bottom of the sloping radiator on the CWA6 projected in front of the dumbirons, causing it to exceed the maximum permitted length for which it required special dispensation. A.B Cross

Although the Brush bodies were very similar in appearance to the Duples, there were several minor differences which helped distinguish them, one of the more prominent being a row of ventilators above the lower deck saloon windows. There were also no rain shields above the fixed windows, the opening window was in the fourth rather than the third bay, the front ventilators were slightly narrower, the bottom edge of the cab door window lined up with those of the lower saloon windows and there was a ledge below the windscreen. These were the first utilities to have the newly authorised deeper indicator box, the bottom of which was masked. D 53, a 1/1D3 is parked on Albert Embankment, one of the central London points used for off-peak parking.
The Omnibus Society

The austerity specification was gradually relaxed as each batch of Daimlers was built and the second Duple highbridge sanction (classified 1/1D2/1) had five opening windows on each side and seats covered in moquette. In contrast, supplies of red paint were again short and they were painted in brown and cream, similar to the later Guys except that the relief colour was applied to the window surrounds on both decks. The first in the batch, D 74, is at Crystal Palace on route 137, a short-lived allocation for the class.
Brian Bunker collection

Chassis:	Daimler CWA6; (D 127, 138–140, 142 CWD6)	
Engine:	AEC A173 direct injection 7.7 litre 86 bhp oil; or	
	Daimler CD6 8.6 litre 100 bhp oil (D 127, 138–140, 142)	
Transmission:	Daimler four speed preselective with fluid flywheel.	
Bodywork:	Duple (D 1–34, 74–92, 128–140, 142); Brush (D 35–73, 93–127);	
Capacity:	UH56R (D 1–6 and 128–131: UL55R)	
L.T. chassis code:	1D (D 1–6); 1/1D (D7–115); 2/1D (D 116–126, 128–137); 2D (127, 138–140, 142).	
L.T. Body codes:	D1 (1–6); D1/1 (128–131); D2 (7–34); D2/1 (74–92); D2/2 (132–140, 142); D3 (35–61); D3/1 (62–73); D3/2 (93–115); D3/3 (116–126); D3/4 (127)	
Built:	1944–1945	
Number built:	141 (still being delivered)	
Number in stock:	1.1.40: Nil	31.12.45: 141

D		Date into stock	D		Date into stock	D		Date into stock
1	GXE578	24.4.44	48	GXV779	13.2.45	95	GYE100	15.5.45
2	GXE579	24.4.44	49	GXV780	14.2.45	96	GYL261	17.5.45
3	GXE580	26.4.44	50	GXV781	16.2.45	97	GYL262	23.5.45
4	GXE581	4.5.44	51	GXV782	16.2.45	98	GYL263	23.5.45
5	GXE582	8.5.44	52	GXV783	26.2.45	99	GYL264	30.5.45
6	GXE583	10.5.44	53	GXV784	27.2.45	100	GYL265	18.5.45
7	GXE584	20.7.44	54	GXV785	26.2.45	101	GYL266	28.5.45
8	GXE585	19.8.44	55	GXV786	7.3.45	102	GYL267	5.6.45
9	GXE586	9.8.44	56	GXV787	14.3.45	103	GYL268	4.6.45
10	GXE587	17.8.44	57	GXV788	8.3.45	104	GYL269	5.6.45
11	GXE588	2.9.44	58	GXV789	28.2.45	105	GYL270	5.6.45
12	GXE589	21.8.44	59	GXV790	15.3.45	106	GYL271	11.6.45
13	GXE590	31.8.44	60	GXV791	13.2.45	107	GYL272	6.6.45
14	GLX900	23.8.44	61	GXV792	16.3.45	108	GYL273	14.6.45
15	GLX901	28.8.44	62	GYE51	19.3.45	109	GYL274	8.6.45
16	GLX902	28.8.44	63	GYE52	11.4.45	110	GYL275	12.6.45
17	GLX903	29.8.44	64	GYE53	27.3.45	111	GYL276	18.6.45
18	GLX904	4.9.44	65	GYE54	28.3.45	112	GYL277	15.6.45
19	GLX905	6.9.44	66	GYE55	9.4.45	113	GYL278	19.6.45
20	GLX906	7.9.44	67	GYE56	12.4.45	114	GYL279	2.7.45
21	GLX907	27.9.44	68	GYE57	17.4.45	115	GYL280	20.6.45
22	GLX908	4.9.44	69	GYE58	16.3.45	116	GYL281	2.7.45
23	GLX909	4.9.44	70	GYE59	27.2.45	117	GYL282	21.6.45
24	GLX910	9.9.44	71	GYE60	1.3.45	118	GYL283	21.6.45
25	GLX911	6.9.44	72	GYE61	20.3.45	119	GYL284	2.7.45
26	GLX912	11.9.44	73	GYE62	13.4.45	120	GYL285	2.7.45
27	GLX913	22.9.44	74	GYE64	6.3.45	121	GYL286	2.7.45
28	GLX914	15.9.44	75	GYE65	22.3.45	122	GYL287	4.7.45
29	GLX915	15.9.44	76	GYE66	21.3.45	123	GYL288	3.7.45
30	GLX916	13.9.44	77	GYE67	24.3.45	124	GYL289	6.7.45
31	GLX917	18.9.44	78	GYE68	23.3.45	125	GYL290	6.7.45
32	GLX918	5.10.44	79	GYE69	7.3.45	126	GYL291	5.7.45
33	GLX919	25.9.44	80	GYE70	8.3.45	127	GYL292	20.8.45
34	GLX920	25.9.44	81	GYE71	9.3.45	128	HGC255	1.11.45
35	GLX921	26.1.45	82	GYE72	10.3.45	129	HGC256	5.11.45
36	GLX922	26.1.45	83	GYE73	12.3.45	130	HGC257	6.11.45
37	GLX923	30.1.45	84	GYE74	13.3.45	131	HGC258	10.11.45
38	GLX924	30.1.45	85	GYE75	27.3.45	132	HGC259	14.11.45
39	GXV770	1.2.45	86	GYE76	15.3.45	133	HGC260	19.11.45
40	GXV771	1.2.45	87	GYE77	16.3.45	134	HGC261	16.11.45
41	GXV772	6.2.45	88	GYE78	17.3.45	135	HGC262	16.11.45
42	GXV773	7.2.45	89	GYE79	19.3.45	136	HGC263	20.11.45
43	GXV774	6.2.45	90	GYE80	20.3.45	137	HGC264	23.11.45
44	GXV775	12.2.45	91	GYE81	5.4.45	138	HGC265	30.11.45
45	GXV776	28.2.45	92	GYE82	29.3.45	139	HGC266	1.12.45
46	GXV777	8.2.45	93	GYE98	12.5.45	140	HGC267	21.12.45
47	GXV778	14.2.45	94	GYE99	15.5.45	142	HGC269	29.12.45

Withdrawn Dennis Darts await their fate in Chiswick Tram Depot, the three nearest the camera being DA 43-45, the Metcalfe-bodied examples acquired from Romford and District and the other an unidentified Chiswick-built version. D.W.K. Jones

DA

The Dennis Dart had been the LGOC's standard small bus between 1930 and 1933 during which forty-two were purchased. DA 1–40 were 7ft 2ins wide Chiswick-bodied eighteen-seaters, but DA 41 and 42 were 6ft 6ins wide seventeen seaters for operation on route 211. Three Metcalfe bodied twenty-seaters were added to the London Transport fleet, numbered DA 43–45, when the business of the Romford and District Omnibus Co. Ltd was acquired in July 1934. The DAs continued as a substantial part of the Central Bus one-man fleet until 1939 when they were replaced either by larger buses or by the new CR class. The last two were delicensed on 1st December 1939 and forty-one remained in stock awaiting disposal at the beginning of 1940.

Chassis: Dennis Dart
Engine: Dennis 6-cylinder 70 bhp petrol
Transmission: Dennis 4-speed crash
Bodywork: DA 1–42 LGOC (Chiswick); DA 43–45 Metcalfe
Capacity: B17F (DA 41–42); B18F (DA 1–40); B20F (DA 43–45)
L.T. chassis codes: 1DA (DA 1–32); 2DA (DA 33–40); 3DA (DA 41, 42)*
L.T. body codes: DA1 (DA 1–20); DA2 (DA 21–32); DA3 (DA 33–40); DA4 (DA 41, 42)*
Built: 1930–1934
Number built: 45;
Number in stock: 1.1.40: 41; Last vehicle in stock: 27.3.40
* Codes were not allocated to DA 43–45

DA		Date out of stock	DA		Date out of stock	DA		Date out of stock
1	GF494	8. 3.40	16	GK3090	2. 3.40	34	GX5326	30. 1.40
2	GF493	4. 3.40	17	GK3100	16. 3.40	35	GX5331	8. 3.40
3	GF492	8. 3.40	18	GK3101	4. 3.40	36	GX5327	27. 3.40
4	GF491	15. 3.40	19	GK3108	12. 3.40	37	GX5332	30. 1.40
5	GF7207	8. 3.40	20	GK3132	13. 3.40	38	GX5333	8. 3.40
6	GF7216	27. 3.40	21	GK5342	8. 3.40	39	JJ4333	8. 3.40
7	GH8078	8. 3.40	22	GK5441	8. 3.40	40	JJ4334	2. 3.40
8	GH8079	8. 3.40	25	GN2146	8. 3.40	41	JJ4373	2. 2.40
9	GH8080	6. 3.40	26	GN4738	5. 3.40	42	JJ4374	15. 3.40
10	GH8081	11. 3.40	27	GN4739	8. 3.40	43	EV4011	19. 3.40
11	GH8082	8. 3.40	28	GN4740	8. 3.40	44	EV5909	5. 3.40
12	GK3049	8. 3.40	30	GN4742	12. 4.40			
13	GK3050	8. 3.40	31	GO618	13. 3.40			
14	GK3070	8. 3.40	32	GO661	8. 3.40			
15	GK3075	4. 3.40	33	GX5325	12. 3.40			

BD

London Transport accumulated a small fleet of Bedfords from sixteen Independent operators in the Country Area whose businesses were acquired under the terms of the London Passenger Transport Act (1933). A total of twenty-seven were owned but this number was never in stock at one time. The last eleven were withdrawn during 1939 but remained in stock at the start of 1940.

Chassis:	Bedford WLB (BD 21: WLG)
Engine:	Bedford 3.18 litre petrol.
Tranmsission:	Bedford 4-speed crash
Bodywork:	Duple (BD 3, 7, 9, 10, 15, 20); Reall (BD 8); Thurgood (BD 17); Not known (1, 21, 23)
Capacity:	B20F; (BD10, 23 C20F)
L.T. chassis codes:	Not allocated
L.T. body codes:	Not allocated
Built:	1931 (BD 21); 1932 (BD 8, 15, 17, 20, 23); 1933 (BD 1, 3, 7, 9, 10)
Number built:	27
Number in stock:	1.1.40: 11; Last vehicle out of stock: 14.2.40

BD		Date out of stock	BD		Date out of stock	BD		Date out of stock
1	AGY485	13. 2.40	9	APB940	14. 2.40	20	MV6324	12. 2.40
3	AKE725	13. 2.40	10	APC55	12. 2.40	21	PJ1727	7. 2.40
7	AMH881	9. 2.40	15	JH974	8. 2.40	23	PJ8430	9. 2.40
8	AMY660	14. 2.40	17	JH2314	7. 2.40			

T 1 was still looking much as it always had, including the original front wheel centres and intact glass louvres over the half-drop windows, when photographed running from Enfield garage on route 205 in the first half of the war. W.J. Haynes

T

The T class was first introduced as a bus by the London General Omnibus Company in 1929, when fifty 30-seaters (T 1–37, 39–50, 156; 1T1 and variations) were put into service. As required by contemporary regulations, they had doorless rear entrances but, between 1933 and 1935 all but five were converted to front entrance. The five which retained their rear entrances were T 15, 21, 25, 26 and 35 (5/1T1/1) which had been transferred to the East Surrey Traction Co. Ltd in 1931, becoming part of the Country Bus fleet when the LPTB was formed. T 43 (2T2) was originally fitted with an experimental eight cylinder engine and when this was replaced by a standard six cylinder unit its wheelbase was shortened and its capacity reduced to twenty-nine.

The only rear-entrance 1T1 still in service at the beginning of 1940 was T 21 which was withdrawn on 30th September 1942. Two others were still in stock, T 15, which was lost when the former Tilling premises at Bull Yard, Peckham, were bombed in 1940; and T 26, which was sold to the War Department in 1940. T 21 was fitted up as a snow plough in November 1942 and remained in this condition until withdrawn and sold to the War Department in 1945. But for the intervention of the war the remaining forty-five, all with front entrances, would have been withdrawn in the early 1940s but all were still in service at the end of 1945. Between November 1940 and January 1944 fifteen 1T1s, still painted red, spent varying amounts of time working in the Country Area, although not all were in service there at the same time. They were Ts 6, 11, 13, 24, 31, 32, 37, 41, 43–48 and 50.

T 38 was a prototype coach for the newly developing suburban coach services (later Green Line) and this was followed by a further 250 (T 51–149, 155, 157–206 with rear entrances – 7T7; 207–306, front entrances – 1/7T7/1). All were withdrawn as coaches with the arrival of the 10T10s and TFs during 1938/1939 but twenty-four 1/7T7/1s had larger indicator boxes fitted and continued in use as buses, replacing other bus Regals in the T 369–390 series. Nineteen 7T7s were returned to bus work at the beginning of the war and some were again used as coaches for a time in 1941 at Amersham, Dunton Green, St Albans and Tunbridge Wells garages (T 51, 56, 61, 66, 94, 108, 109, 111, 113, 114, 118, 121, 124, 132, 136, 145, 180, 182, 184). All were withdrawn again by 1942 but were brought back into use as snow ploughs in 1944 before being withdrawn finally in 1945.

All 1T1s originally had open rear platforms but the only survivors in 1940 were three of the five Country Buses which had never been modified. Of these only T 21 remained in service and it was photographed in Clarendon Road, Redhill in March 1941, eighteen months before it was finally withdrawn. Ken Glazier collection

Sixteen of the withdrawn 1/7T7/1 coaches were taken from store and converted to staff ambulances in September 1939, for which purpose the rear emergency door was widened by increasing the pillar spacing (T 209, 219, 229, 249, 252, 258, 262, 264, 265, 270, 277, 290, 292, 297, 301, 302). They were renumbered into the service vehicle series. The body of T 258 was damaged by enemy action in September 1940 and its chassis was used to replace a Regal lorry which had also been bombed. To make up the number of staff ambulances, T 120 was converted. The ambulances were all converted back to buses, having their indicator boxes enlarged during the second half of 1945, when T 120 had its rear entrance body replaced by a front entrance example off T 305. T 231, 235 and 273 were transferred to Central Buses and repainted red in February 1945. The nineteen 7T7s and sixteen of the 1/7T7/1s were sold in May 1945 to the War Department for use by the Control Commission in Germany, leaving T 120 as the sole 7T and twenty-three 1/7T7/1s in stock at the end of 1945.

Thomas Tilling Ltd also purchased twelve Regals in 1932 (T 307–318; 3T3) for operation on route 109 (renumbered 227 in 1934). They had Tilling's own distinctive style of twenty-eight seat front entrance bodywork (later increased to thirty), based on their contemporary double-deck design, with a wider and shallower destination blind box than the LGOC version. London Transport replaced them at Bromley by the larger LTL and transferred them to Kingston garage.

London Transport acquired sixty-three other Regals from a variety of sources, twenty-two buses and forty-one coaches. Some came by direct acquisition from Independent operators and others from or via Green Line Coaches Ltd and London General Country Services Ltd. Of the coaches (T 319–324, 346–368, 391–402), only two Dodson-bodied thirty-seaters which had been acquired from Bucks Expresses by Green Line Coaches Ltd in 1932 remained in their original condition at the beginning of 1940 (T 391 and 392; 2/8T8/4). Twelve others (T 346–357; classified 5T4) had been rebodied in 1935 with new Weymann twenty-nine seat bus bodies, similar to the type fitted to AEC Reliance chassis that year; T 396 was the prototype for the 11T11 modernisation programme described below; T 359, 361, 362 and 364 were included in that programme; and the rest were withdrawn. Of the twenty-two buses (T 369–390), eight remained in stock in 1940, six rear entrance thirty-seaters (T 375–377, 383–385; 4/1T6) and one front entrance (T 382; 4/1T6) all formerly London General Country Services vehicles; and T 369, formerly Watford Bus Company, which had been fitted with a T7/1 coach body in 1938. All twelve 5T4s, six of the Country Bus rear entrance buses, T 382 and T 392 were sold in 1945 to the War Department for use by the Control Commission in Germany, leaving only Ts 369 and 391 still owned at the end of 1945.

In 1936 the LPTB purchased fifty Weymann bodied Regals for Green Line service (T 403–452; classified 9T9). These were London's first Regals with oil engines, pre-selective gearboxes and fluid flywheels. Their Weymann bodies set a new standard in design which was to be the basis of all subsequent pre-war single-deckers. The 9T9s were demoted to bus work in 1939. As part of its large 1938/39 replacement programme London Transport ordered 266 AEC Regals (the 10T10 class) to replace all pre-1936 Green Line coaches. These employed the new AEC pot cavity 8.8 litre oil engine, which had been inspired by the similar engines supplied by Leyland in the STD class. The bodywork was of composite construction, the first run of such bodies built in the shops at Chiswick. The first 150 had thirty seats but the last 116 were to a modified design with thirty-four seats.

In 1938, when the R-class chassis were scrapped, their 1935 Weymann 30-seat bodies were salvaged and mounted on the chassis of thirty-one withdrawn Regal coaches which were fitted with 7.7 litre oil engines at the same time and reclassified 11T11. All were originally Country Buses but eleven were repainted red between 1939 and 1945 for operation first on route 211 (Hanwell garage) and later route 221 (Harrow Weald).

There were also three vehicles which were not AEC Regals but were included in the class by the LGOC for convenience (T 1000–1002; classified CB). These had experimental chassis built by the LGOC in 1931, part of an aborted project which was also intended to encompass vehicles similar to the ST and LT classes but, apart from the Ts, extended only to four LTs. All three Ts were withdrawn in 1939 and were sold in August 1940.

At the outbreak of war Green Line services were suspended and all 9T9s and 10T10s were converted to public ambulances for use in the evacuation of hospital patients from London and during the expected air bombardment. All but fifty-five of the 10T10 ambulances were restored to passenger service in September and November 1939, when a start was made on restoring most Green Line services. A total of six 9T9s and eighty-eight 10T10s was seconded for active wartime service with the American armed forces between September 1942 and June 1943 and stayed with them until the end of hostilities. The 9T9s and twenty-four of the 10T10s were used as transports by the US Army and nine 10T10s in the same role by the American Red Cross. Fifty-five of the 10T10s were converted by Elliott's of Reading for use by the American Red Cross as mobile canteens, known as 'Clubmobiles'. The conversion included the installation of a serving counter on the offside, tables and chairs and a cooker. There was also a separate compartment with two beds for the operators. Twelve 10T10s and one 9T9 did not return from war service, the fate of most of them being unknown, but at least two found their way to other operators. T 460 went to D.J. Davies of Merthyr (registered HB6138) and T 594 to Smith of Reading (BRD922). The remainder, twenty of which had yet to be returned at the end of 1945, and the public ambulances re-entered passenger service in 1945/1946. The 10T10s which remained in passenger service after 1942 were used as buses throughout the Country Area until the end of the war.

In 1941/1942 thirty-one 1T1s, ten 10T10s, forty-eight 1/11T10/1s, all the Tillings, nine ST4s and twenty-two 11T11s had their seating re-arranged around the perimeter to create space for twenty standing passengers. Most of those still in stock at the end of 1945 were still in this condition. Another wartime novelty was that twenty-eight Ts, including the nineteen 7T7 coaches, were converted for use as snow ploughs for varying periods between November 1942 and May 1945, after which they were withdrawn for disposal.

The T class made a small contribution to the fleet of producer gas vehicles which operated between December 1942 and September 1944. T 273 was the first, being licensed at Grays in October 1942, and eight more followed: T 288, 347, 350, 352, 353,

Top **The former Thomas Tilling 3T3s had very distinctive bodywork, similar in style and finish to their contemporary STLs, the most immediate point of recognition being the wide indicator boxes. They spent most of their London Transport careers allocated to Kingston, where T 314 was photographed alongside the coal yard.** W.J. Haynes

Above **T 385B was a Hall Lewis thirty-seat rear-entrance bus, classified 4/1T6, which had been new to East Surrey Traction in 1930.** A.B. Cross

354, 355 and 357. T 273 and 288 were reclassified 12T7/2 and the remainder, all from the batch with Weymann 1935 bodies, 13T4/1. All nine were eventually allocated to Addlestone and Leatherhead garages for route 462 where they operated from June 1943 until being restored to petrol propulsion in August/September 1944. T 10 may also have been equipped but did not operate as a gas bus.

The 5T4 class was very similar in appearance to the better known 11T11s because they carried the same type of handsome Weymann bodywork dating from 1935. The 5T4s were formerly coaches acquired from Blue Belle Motors and Queen Line Coaches, which, although rebodied retained their petrol engines and were therefore withdrawn and sold in 1945. T 354B is seen at work from Windsor garage before it became one of the nine Ts converted for producer gas operation between 1942 and 1944. Frank Willis

Twenty-four 1/7T7/1 former Green Line coaches had been converted for use as buses when they were displaced from coach work in 1938/1939. Apart from the change of fleet name, they were also given larger indicator boxes with a standard size aperture. T 233B has also been repainted into the wartime green and white style. D.W.K. Jones

Despite being downgraded to bus status when replaced by 10T10s, the 9T9s were nevertheless drafted as public ambulances on the outbreak of war. Judging from the absence of headlamp masks, this photograph of T 408B, one of a number of coaches allotted to Chalk Farm garage, was taken in 1945, after the lifting of blackout restrictions. Characteristics of the 9T9 not shared by the otherwise very similar 10T10 were the incorporation of the headlamp into the wing assembly, the extension of the wing panelling to cover the dumbirons, the bumper bar, the internally sliding platform door and the gradual curve of the roof moulding into the front dome. They also had a longer wheelbase and, in consequence, a shorter rear overhang. R.H.G. Simpson

The many 10T10s which were used as buses during the war years were repainted in the new Lincoln green and white livery displayed by T 651, a thirty-four seat 1/10T10/1 which has also lost its rear wheel trim discs. Malcolm Papes collection

Chassis:	AEC Regal 662/0662
Engine:	AEC A140 6-cylinder 6.1 litre 95 bhp petrol (T 1–50, 156, 369); AEC A145 6-cylinder 7.4 litre 95 bhp petrol (T 51–392 range except 156, 369 and 11T11 type);
	AEC A173 6-cylinder 7.7 litre direct injection 95 bhp oil (11T11 class – see fleet list);
	AEC A171 6-cylinder 7.7 litre 95 bhp oil (T 403–452); AEC A180 6-cylinder 8.8 litre direct injection 100 bhp oil (T 453–718).
Transmission:	AEC D124 four speed crash (T 1–396 range); AEC D132 four-speed direct selection preselective with fluid flywheel (T 403–718).
Bodywork:	LGOC (T 1–50, 156); LGOC, Short Bros or Hall Lewis (T 51–184 range, except 120, 156), Weymann, Ransomes or Duple (T 207–306 range); Hall Lewis (T 375–377, 383–385); Weymann (11T11 type, T 346–357, 382, 403–452); Dodson (T 391, 392), LPTB (T 453–718);
Capacity*:	B27F (T 51–184 range, except 120, 346–357, 369); B28F (T 307–319); B30F (T 1–14, 16–20, 22–24, 27–34, 36, 37, 39–50, 403–452); B30R (T 15, 21, 25, 26, 35, 375–377, 383–385); DP30 or 34F (T 453–718).
L.T. codes:	1, 1/1 or 2/1T1 or 1/1 (T 1–50, 156); 4/1T6 (T 375–377, 382–385); 3T3 (307–318); 5T4 (T 346–357); 7T7 (T 51–184 range except 120, 156); 1/7T7/1 (T 120, 207–305 range, 369); 2/8T8/4 (T 391, 392); 9T9 (T 403–452); 1/10 or 10T/T10 or 10/1 (T 453–718); 11T11 (see below).
Built:	1929 (T 1–50); 1930/31 (T 51–305 range, 375–377, 382–385, 391, 392); 1930/31 chassis/1935 body (11T11 type – marked * in list and T 346–357); 1932 (T 307–318, 369); 1936 (403–452); 1938/39 (493–717).
Number built:	700 (to end 1945)
Number in stock:	1.1.40: 478 31.12.45: 397
	* When modified for standee operation the seating capacities were: 1T1 and 10T10 – 29; 3T3 – 28; 5T4 and 11T11 – 27; 1/10T10/1 – 30 (all plus twenty standing).

T		Date out of stock	T		Date out of stock	T		Date out of stock
1	UU6616		†145	GF517	1.5.45	274	GN2177	
2	UU6617		156	GF7251		*275	GK3177	
3	UU6618		159	GF588	25.2.40 s	*276	GH3825	
4	UU6619		160	GF573	20.9.40 s	277	GK3180	
5	UU6620		163	GH614	20.8.40 s	*280	GN4647	
6	UU6621		164	GF591	22.8.40 s	281	GK3171	2.5.45
7	UU6622		165	GF574	17.7.40 s	*283	GN2104	
8	UU6623		167	GH3887	17.7.40 s	*285	GH8098	
9	UU6624		169	GH3886	24.8.40 s	286	GN2179	16.5.45
10	UU6625		171	GH3882	19.8.40 s	288	GN2103	16.5.45
11	UU6626		172	GH3883	20.9.40 s	290	GN2106	
12	UU6627		174	GH8003	26.8.40 s	291	GN2105	16.5.45
13	UU6628		175	GH8005	8.8.40 s	292	GN2108	
14	UU6629		176	GH8001	20.9.40 s	†293	GK5499	2.5.45
15	UU6630	22.10.40 b	178	GH8004	1.3.40 s	295	GN4682	3.5.45
16	UU6631		†180	GH612	2.5.45	*296	GN4684	
17	UU6632		181	GH616	17.9.40 s	297	GN2107	
18	UU6633		†182	GH3814	3.5.45	*298	GN4672	
19	UU6634		†184	GH618	1.5.45	301	GK3173	
20	UU6635		199	GH620	21.10.40 s	302	GN4671	
†21	UU6636	1.5.45	203	GH8094	6.8.40 s	†305	GN2178	
22	UU6637		206	GH3819	8.8.40 s	306	GN4673	4.3.40
23	UU6638		207	GK5493		307	GY8419	
24	UU6639		* 208	GH8096		308	GY8408	
26	UU6641	12.1.40	209	GK5490		309	GY8409	
27	UU6642		211	GK5487	16.5.45	310	GY8410	
28	UU6643		*212	GK5492		311	GY8411	
29	UU6644		*213	GN2016		312	GY8412	
30	UU6645		*214	GK3181		313	GY8413	
31	UU6646		*215	GK5488		314	GY8414	
32	UU6647		*216	GN2176		315	GY8415	
33	UU6648		217	GN2002	16.5.45	316	GY8416	
34	UU6649		218	GK3183	1.5.45	317	GY8417	
36	UU6651		219	GK5486		318	GY8418	
37	UU6652		*223	GK5491		346	GF5135	2.5.45
39	UU6654		*226	GN2018		347	GF5136	1.5.45
40	UU6655		229	GK5494		348	GJ8068	3.5.45
41	UU6656		230	GH5495		349	GJ8069	3.5.45
42	UU6657		231	GH3805		350	GJ8072	2.5.45
43	UU6658		*232	GH3803		351	GJ8073	3.5.45
44	UU6659		233	GK3188	3.5.45	352	GN4416	1.5.45
45	UU6660		*234	GK3185		353	GN8238	1.5.45
46	UU6661		235	GK3186	2.5.45	354	GN8239	1.5.45
47	UU6662		*236	GN2080		355	GN8240	1.5.45
48	UU6663		*237	GN2004		356	GN8241	3.5.45
49	UU6664		239	GN2005	3.5.45	357	GN8242	3.5.45
50	UU6665		240	GN2020		*359	KX7886	
†51	GF526	1.5.45	244	GH3888		*361	KX7634	
†56	GF540	2.5.45	248	GN2017	3.5.45	*362	KX7635	
†61	GF538	3.5.45	249	GK3190		*364	KX6785	
†66	GF501	3.5.45	*250	GN2069		369	JH2101	
76	GF521	26.2.40	251	GH3889		375	PG7507	12.1.40
85	GF7278	26.2.40	252	GH3801		†376	PG7508	3.5.45
†94	GF580	2.5.45	*253	GH3807		†377	PG7509	1.5.45
101	GF582	26.2.40	254	GH3806		†382	PL6458	1.5.45
†108	GF586	1.5.45	*255	GK5497		†383	PG6783	2.5.45
†109	GF599	1.5.45	*261	GN2023		†384	PG6784	3.5.45
†111	GF551	2.5.45	262	GH3890		†385	PG6785	2.5.45
†113	GF7280	2.5.45	263	GK3175	3.5.45	391	JH32	
†114	GF587	3.5.45	264	GH3820		392	JH33	2.5.45
116	GF509	26.2.40	265	GH3823		*396	PG7839	
118	GF502	2.5.45	*266	GK3187		403	CLX551	
120	GF557		*267	GH3824		404	CLX552	
†121	GF594	3.5.45	270	GH3821		405	CLX553	
†124	GF568	1.5.45	*271	GH3822		406	CLX554	
†132	GF566	2.5.45	272	GH8099	2.5.45	407	CLX555	
†136	GF545	3.5.45	273	GN4683		408	CLX556	

b Destroyed by bombing   * 11T11   † Fitted with snow ploughs at various times between 1942 and 1944
s Converted to open lorry on date shown   The numbers T 325–345 were never used

T		Date out of stock	Date returned	T		Date out of stock	Date returned
409	CLX557			476	ELP200		
410	CLX558			477	ELP201		
411	CLX559			478	ELP202		
412	CLX560			479	ELP203	15.2.43	9.11.45
413	CLX561			480	ELP204		
414	CLX562	30.10.42	26.11.45	481	ELP205		
415	CLX563	30.10.42	30.11.45	482	ELP206		
416	CLX564	30.10.42	26.11.45	483	ELP207		
417	CLX565			484	ELP208		
418	CLX566			485	ELP209		
419	CLX567			486	ELP210	22.12.42	n
420	CLX568			487	ELP211		
421	CLX569	30.10.42		488	ELP212	16.9.42	n
422	CLX570	30.10.42		489	ELP213		
423	CLX571			490	ELP214	30.10.42	30.11.45
424	CLX572			491	ELP215		
425	CLX573			492	ELP216	16.9.42	
426	CLX574			493	ELP217		
427	CLX575			494	ELP218		
428	CXX151			495	ELP219		
429	CXX152			496	ELP220		
430	CXX153			497	ELP221		
431	CXX154			498	ELP222		
432	CXX155			499	ELP223		
433	CXX156			500	ELP224		
434	CXX157			501	ELP225		
435	CXX158			502	ELP226		
436	CXX159			503	ELP227		
437	CXX160			504	ELP228		
438	CXX161			505	ELP229		
439	CXX162			506	ELP230		
440	CXX163			507	ELP231		
441	CXX164			508	ELP232		
442	CXX165			509	ELP233	22.12.42	n
443	CXX166	30.10.42	n	510	ELP234	1.2.43	5.11.45
444	CXX167			511	ELP235		
445	CXX168			512	ELP236		
446	CXX169			513	ELP237		
447	CXX170			514	ELP238		
448	CXX171			515	ELP239		
449	CXX172			516	ELP240		
450	CXX173			517	ELP241		
451	CXX174			518	ELP242		
452	CXX175			519	ELP243		
453	ELP177			520	ELP244		
454	ELP178			521	ELP245		
455	ELP179	30.10.42		522	ELP246		
456	ELP180			523	ELP247		
457	ELP181	30.10.42		524	ELP248	16.9.42	23.11.45
458	ELP182			525	ELP249		
459	ELP183			526	ELP250		
460	ELP184	30.10.42	n	527	ELP251		
461	ELP185			528	ELP252		
462	ELP186	22.12.42		529	ELP253		
463	ELP187	22.12.42		530	ELP254	12.2.43	16.11.45
464	ELP188			531	ELP255		
465	ELP189	25.1.43	26.11.45	532	ELP256		
466	ELP190			533	ELP257		
467	ELP191			534	ELP258		
468	ELP192			535	ELP259	25.1.43	16.11.45
469	ELP193			536	ELP260		
470	ELP194			537	ELP261		
471	ELP195			538	ELP262	10.2.43	5.11.45
472	ELP196			539	ELP263		
473	ELP197			540	ELP264		
474	ELP198			541	ELP265		
475	ELP199			542	ELP266		

The dates refer to the period during which the coaches were seconded to the US Army or American Red Cross
n Not returned after use by US Army

T		Date out of stock	Date returned		T		Date out of stock	Date returned
543	ELP267				610	EYK245		
544	ELP268	10.2.43	9.11.45		611	EYK246		
545	ELP269				612	EYK247	18.1.43	
546	ELP270	22.12.42	27.12.45		613	EYK248		
547	ELP271	22.12.42			614	EYK249		
548	ELP272				615	EYK250	21.1.43	9.11.45
549	ELP273	25.1.43	9.11.45		616	EYK251		
550	ELP274				617	EYK252		
551	ELP275	19.1.43	21.11.45		618	EYK253		
552	ELP276				619	EYK254		
553	ELP277				620	EYK255		
554	ELP278				621	EYK256		
555	ELP279				622	EYK257		
556	ELP280				623	EYK258		
557	ELP281				624	EYK259		
558	ELP282				625	EYK260		
559	ELP283				626	EYK261		
560	ELP284				627	EYK262		
561	ELP285	1.2.43	26.11.45		628	EYK263	18.1.43	22.11.45
562	ELP286				629	EYK264		
563	ELP287				630	EYK265	9.1.43	26.11.45
564	ELP288				631	EYK266		
565	ELP289	1.2.43	16.11.45		632	EYK267	15.2.43	9.11.45
566	EYK201	16.9.42			633	EYK268	12.2.43	22.11.45
567	EYK202	25.1.43	29.10.45		634	EYK269		
568	EYK203				635	EYK270	15.1.43	16.11.45
569	EYK204	22.12.42			636	EYK271		
570	EYK205				637	EYK272	18.6.43	16.11.45
571	EYK206				638	EYK273		
572	EYK207	16.9.42			639	EYK274	18.1.43	5.11.45
573	EYK208				640	EYK275	14.1.43	22.11.45
574	EYK209				641	EYK276		
575	EYK210				642	EYK277		
576	EYK211				643	EYK278		
577	EYK212				644	EYK279		
578	EYK213	16.9.42	n		645	EYK280		
579	EYK214				646	EYK281	23.1.43	5.11.45
580	EYK215				647	EYK282		
581	EYK216				648	EYK283	22.6.43	
582	EYK217	16.9.42	23.11.45		649	EYK284	4.1.43	16.11.45
583	EYK218				650	EYK285	15.1.43	21.11.45
584	EYK219				651	EYK286		
585	EYK220				652	EYK287	17.6.43	16.11.45
586	EYK221	16.9.42	n		653	EYK288		
587	EYK222	22.12.42	n		654	EYK289	12.2.43	21.11.45
588	EYK223				655	EYK290		
589	EYK224				656	EYK291	18.6.43	5.11.45
590	EYK225	22.12.42			657	EYK292		
591	EYK226				658	EYK293		
592	EYK227	16.9.42			659	EYK294	15.2.43	16.11.45
593	EYK228				660	EYK295	19.1.43	11.11.45
594	EYK229	16.9.42			661	EYK296		
595	EYK230				662	EYK297	20.1.43	9.11.45
596	EYK231				663	EYK298	27.5.43	4.12.45
597	EYK232				664	EYK299		
598	EYK233				665	EYK300	17.6.43	n
599	EYK234				666	EYK301	18.1.43	n
600	EYK235				667	EYK302		
601	EYK236	21.1.43	16.11.45		668	EYK303	17.6.43	9.11.45
602	EYK237				669	EYK304	23.1.43	22.11.45
603	EYK238	12.2.43	22.11.45		670	EYK305	22.6.43	n
604	EYK239				671	EYK306		
605	EYK240	22.12.42	4.12.45		672	EYK307		
606	EYK241				673	EYK308	17.6.43	21.11.45
607	EYK242				674	EYK309	18.6.43	9.11.45
608	EYK243				675	EYK310		
609	EYK244	22.1.43	9.11.45		676	EYK311		

The dates refer to the period during which the coaches were seconded to the US Army or American Red Cross
n Not returned after use by US Army

T		Date out of stock	Date returned	T		Date out of stock	Date returned
677	EYK312			698	EYK333		
678	EYK313			699	EYK334		
679	EYK314			700	EYK335		
680	EYK315	17.6.43	15.1.46	701	EYK336	16.6.43	5.11.45
681	EYK316	16.2.43	n	702	EYK337	15.1.43	9.11.45
682	EYK317	13.1.43	16.11.45	703	EYK338	4.1.43	9.11.45
683	EYK318	18.6.43	9.11.45	704	EYK339		
684	EYK319	27.5.43	30.11.45	705	EYK340	17.6.43	9.11.45
685	EYK320	20.1.43	16.11.45	706	EYK341		
686	EYK321	17.6.43	5.11.45	707	EYK342		
687	EYK322			708	EYK343	18.1.43	16.11.45
688	EYK323	16.2.43	27.12.43	709	EYK344		
689	EYK324	16.6.43	21.11.45	710	EYK345	17.6.43	16.11.45
690	EYK325			711	EYK346		
691	EYK326			712	EYK347	16.6.43	5.11.45
692	EYK327			713	EYK348		
693	EYK328			714	EYK349		
694	EYK329			715	EYK350	21.6.43	
695	EYK330	9.1.43		716	EYK351		
696	EYK331	20.1.43	21.11.45	717	EYK352	27.5.43	
697	EYK332			718	EYK353	27.5.43	

The dates refer to the period during which the coaches were seconded to the US Army or American Red Cross
n Not returned after use by US Army

* 11T11
† Fitted with snow ploughs at various times between 1942 and 1944
b Destroyed by bombing
s Converted to open lorry on date shown

The following vehicles were temporarily converted to staff ambulances during the war, when the following service vehicle numbers were allocated:

T 120 456W	T 262 435W	T 292 432W
T 209 431W	T 264 425W	T 297 427W
T 219 428W	T 265 433W	T 301 423W
T 229 430W	T 270 429W	T 302 437W
T 249 438W	T 277 434W	
T 252 424W	T 290 426W	

The following vehicles were converted to open lorries on the dates shown in the fleet list were allocated the following numbers in the service vehicle series:

T 159 420W	T 171 447W	T 199 450W
T 160 451W	T 172 453W	T 203 441W
T 163 445W	T 174 449W	T 206 443W
T 164 444W	T 175 442W	
T 165 439W	T 176 452W	
T 167 440W	T 178 421W	
T 169 448W	T 181 446W	

GREEN LINE COACHES SECONDED TO THE US ARMY 1942–1945

The 9T9 and 10T10 coaches which went to the United States Army were each allocated a number by the military authorities and those which became American Red Cross 'Clubmobiles' were also given names. The 'Clubmobiles' were:

X201001	T 465	South Dakota		X201029	T 609	South Carolina
X201002	T 551	Utah		X201030	T 650	Kansas
X201003	T 601	Montana		X201031	T 479	Maryland
X201004	T 630	Pennsylvania		X201032	T 530	Connecticut
X201005	T 695	New York		X201033	T 549	Washington
X201006	T 703	Ohio		X201034	T 633	Colorado
X201007	T 682	Illinois		X201035	T 567	Nebraska
X201008	T 640	Texas		X201036	T 702	Maine
X201009	T 649	California		X201037	T 603	Oregon
X201010	T 708	Massachusetts		X201038	T 685	Columbia
X201011	T 669	Michigan		X201039	T 635	Rhode Island
X201012	T 615	Missouri		X201040	T 535	North Dakota
X201013	T 646	New Jersey		X201103	T 680	Milwaukee
X201014	T 662	Indiana		X201104	T 705	San Francisco
X201015	T 565	North Carolina		X201105	T 710	Boston
X201016	T 660	Georgia		X201106	T 701	Newark
X201017	T 510	Wisconsin		X201107	T 689	Minneapolis
X201018	T 696	Kentucky		X201108	T 712	Houston
X201019	T 561	Tennessee		X201109	T 673	Buffalo
X201020	T 666	Minnesota		X201110	T 665	Rochester
X201021	T 538	Alabama		X201111	T 686	Indeanapolis
X201022	T 639	Louisiana		X201112	T 652	Seattle
X201023	T 544	Iowa		X201113	T 668	Kansas City
X201024	T 628	Mississippi		X201114	T 683	Cincinnatti
X201025	T 659	Oklahoma		X201115	T 637	New Orleans
X201026	T 612	West Virginia		X201116	T 656	New Hampshire
X201027	T 632	Arkansas		X201117	T 674	Baltimore
X201028	T 654	Florida				

The coaches used by the American Red Cross as transports were numbered as follows:

X201041	T 688		X201122	T 663
X201042	T 681		X201123	T 648
X201119	T 715		X201124	T 718
X201120	T 670		X201125	T 717
X201121	T 684			

The vehicles used by the US Army as transports were allocated the following army numbers:

1823725	T 524		1824022	T 414
1823727	T 492		1824023	T 416
1823728	T 592		1824026	T 422
1823729	T 566		1824027	T 421
1823730	T 488		1824048	T 462
1823731	T 572		1824049	T 605
1823733	T 582		1824050	T 569
1824018	T 415		1824052	T 547
1824020	T 455		1824054	T 546
1824021	T 490		1824056	T 590

The US Army numbers of the following vehicles are not known: T 443, 457, 460, 463, 486, 509, 578, 586, 587, 594

The single-deck Renowns were a lengthened version of the 1T1 type Regal but had always had front entrances. LT 1026, seen at Belmont Road Wallington, was a 1LTL1, the type without a rear destination blind box. W.J. Haynes

LT

There were originally 201 single-deck LTs, 199 delivered to the LGOC during 1931 (LT 1001–1050, 1052–1136, 1138–1201; 1/LTL/1 or 1/1) and two to London General Country Services Ltd in 1932 (LT 1427, 1428; 2LTL3), all to the same basic specification. There was also a solitary coach which was acquired with the business of Edward Hillman's Saloon Coaches in 1934 (LT 1429; 3LTL4). The LTL was the most numerous single-deck type in the Central Bus fleet, covering two-thirds of the scheduled large saloon operations. All 202 were still in stock at the beginning of 1940 but a number, including Country Bus LTs 1427 and 1428 and private hire coach LT 1429, were in store.

During the war the number of buses needed for service in the Central Area was reduced, and nine red LTLs were lent to the Country Bus department for a time in 1941 and 1942. LT 1040 and 1044 were short-term loans which operated at Watford for six months in 1941 but the remaining seven (LT 1080, 1083, 1162, 1175, 1176, 1198 and 1200) stayed until 30th September 1942 for operation on routes 342 (Hertford) and 355 (St Albans). They were joined by Country Bus LTs 1427 and 1428. Seventy-two of the Central Bus LTLs had their seating re-arranged longitudinally around the perimeter of the saloon to provide space for twenty standees, the number of seats being reduced to thirty-three. Most of the modifications were made between December 1941 and September 1942, the last of a few stragglers being completed in 1944. Most were still in this condition at the end of 1945.

Withdrawal of the oldest LTs should have started in 1940 but the embargo on new vehicle construction during the Second World War extended the lives of most of them by up to twelve years. The first losses from the class occurred when all eleven stored vehicles were destroyed in the bombing of the former Tilling premises at Bull Yard, Peckham in October 1940. One other bus was lost at Elmers End in 1944 when the garage was destroyed by a flying bomb. The rest of the class was still in use in the Central Area at the end of 1945, LT 1427 and 1428 having been transferred to Central Buses in 1944.

LT 1060, a 1LTL1/1 negotiates the low bridge at Worcester Park station, one of three that determined the need for single-deckers on route 213. On LTL1 bodies, which were the majority, a wooden destination board was carried in slots at the bottom of the window of the rear emergency door. The Omnibus Society

Chassis:	AEC Renown 664
Engine:	AEC A140 6-cylinder 6.1 litre 95 bhp petrol
Transmission:	AEC D124 4 speed crash
Bodywork:	LGOC (Chiswick), except LT 1429: Harrington
Capacity:	B35F*, (LT 1429 C32F)
L.T. chassis code:	1LTL (LT 1001–1201 range); 2LTL (LT 1427, 1428); 3LTL (LT 1429)
L.T. Body codes:	LTL1, 1/1 (LT 1001–1201 range); LTL3 (LT 1427, 1428); LTL4 (LT 1429)
Built:	1931–1932
Number built:	202
Number in stock:	1.1.40: 202 31.12.45: 190
	* Buses converted for standee operation were B33+20F

LT		Date out of stock	LT		Date out of stock	LT		Date out of stock
1001	GH8049		1070	GO5186	22.10.40 b	1139	GP3433	
1002	GN4775		1071	GO5174		1140	GP3422	
1003	GN4776		1072	GO7103		1141	GP3431	
1004	GO605		1073	GO5196		1142	GP3454	
1005	GO601		1074	GO5197		1143	GP3438	
1006	GN4784		1075	GO5199		1144	GP3434	
1007	GO606		1076	GO5198		1145	GP3437	
1008	GN4763		1077	GO7104		1146	GP3439	22.10.40 b
1009	GN4783		1078	GO7141		1147	GP3436	
1010	GO637		1079	GO7102		1148	GP3448	
1011	GN4777		1080	GO7151		1149	GP3457	
1012	GO625		1081	GO7121		1150	GP3455	
1013	GO5114		1082	GO7116		1151	GP3485	22.10.40 b
1014	GO614		1083	GO7119		1152	GT5005	
1015	GO648		1084	GO7129	22.10.40 b	1153	GT5002	
1016	GN4785		1085	GO7125		1154	GT5004	
1017	GO617		1086	GO7142		1155	GT5008	
1018	GO688		1087	GO7120		1156	GT5014	
1019	GO626		1088	GO7117	22.10.40 b	1157	GT5003	
1020	GO5113	22.10.40 b	1089	GO7118		1158	GT5006	
1021	GO607	26.8.44 b	1090	GO7128		1159	GT5015	
1022	GO641		1091	GO7135		1160	GT5007	
1023	GO631		1092	GO7148		1161	GT5013	
1024	GO630		1093	GO7149		1162	GT5016	
1025	GO650		1094	GO7145		1163	GT5022	
1026	GO689		1095	GO5200		1164	GT5030	
1027	GO649		1096	GO7152		1165	GT5029	
1028	GO629		1097	GO7155		1166	GT5028	
1029	GO644		1098	GO7144		1167	GT5027	
1030	GO628		1099	GO7146		1168	GT5033	
1031	GO638		1100	GO7147		1169	GT5031	
1032	GO640	22.10.40 b	1101	GO7150		1170	GT5032	
1033	GO627		1102	GO7161		1171	GT5034	
1034	GO655		1103	GO7165		1172	GT5046	
1035	GO642		1104	GO7159		1173	GT5052	
1036	GO639		1105	GO7163		1174	GT5047	
1037	GO672		1106	GO7167		1175	GT5044	
1038	GO643	22.10.40 b	1107	GO7171		1176	GT5045	
1039	GO668	22.10.40 b	1108	GO7166		1177	GT5054	
1040	GO656		1109	GO7158		1178	GT5053	
1041	GO684		1110	GO7162		1179	GT5059	
1042	GO671		1111	GO7160		1180	GT5060	
1043	GO666		1112	GO7172		1181	GT5061	
1044	GO669		1113	GO7173		1182	GT5079	
1045	GO651		1114	GO7186		1183	GT5062	
1046	GO667		1115	GO7181		1184	GT5074	
1047	GO673		1116	GO7179		1185	GT5072	
1048	GO670		1117	GO7184		1186	GT5080	
1049	GO665		1118	GO7180		1187	GT5075	
1050	GO685		1119	GO7177		1188	GT5076	
1052	GO5159		1120	GO7178		1189	GT5077	
1053	GO5169		1121	GO7185		1190	GT5078	
1054	GO5171	22.10.40. b	1122	GO7192		1191	GT5098	
1055	GO5161		1123	GP3402		1192	GT5090	
1056	GO5160		1124	GP3421		1193	GT5083	
1057	GO5162		1125	GP3401		1194	GT5145	
1058	GO5165		1126	GP3403		1195	GT5094	
1059	GO5170		1127	GP3406		1196	GT5107	
1060	GO5166		1128	GP3405		1197	GT5100	
1061	GO5167		1129	GP3404		1198	GT5101	
1062	GO5178		1130	GO7200		1199	GT5102	
1063	GO5173		1131	GP3407		1200	GT5108	
1064	GO5176		1132	GP3432		1201	GT5120	
1065	GO5187		1133	GP3425		1427	GX5337	
1066	GO5175		1134	GP3430		1428	GX5338	
1067	GO5185		1135	GP3435		1429	EV7340	22.10.40 b
1068	GO5192		1136	GP3420				
1069	GO5177		1138	GP3429				

b Destroyed by bombing

The roofs of the Birmingham Railway Carriage and Wagon Company bodies on the 4Q4s had a distinctive downward slope from front to rear as can be seen in this view of Q 26 on the Castle Hill stand at Windsor. The nearside aspect was reasonably harmonious but the offside was a muddle of different size windows and an emergency door. The fully fronted design required a different approach to the placing of the white blackout markings, otherwise the bus is still in pre-war livery. The bus behind is CR 16B, then almost new.
Ken Glazier collection

Q

The AEC 'Q' was first introduced experimentally by the London General Omnibus Company in 1932 with single-deck Q 1 and the type was for a short period in 1935/36 London Transport's standard single-deck bus. There were five double-deckers but the 232 production vehicles were all single-deckers. London Transport's first order for large saloons was for one hundred centre entrance Qs for the Country Bus department (Q 6–105; coded 4Q4), to which two were added shortly afterwards (Q 187/188). These had Birmingham Railway Carriage & Wagon Company Ltd bodywork seating thirty-seven, two of which were alongside the driver but were found to obstruct the driver's view so were removed during 1936 and replaced by a full width driver's cab. The first London Transport saloons for Central Buses were eighty Qs with a shorter wheelbase so that a doorless entrance could be placed ahead of the front axle. The thirty-seven seat bodywork was supplied by Park Royal and the vehicles were classified 5Q5. Only fifty-three were red, because the last twenty-seven to be built were diverted to the Country Bus department to release a like number of 4Q4s which were modified for Green Line service at the end of 1936. These were reclassified 1/4Q4/1 and retained this coding when they were returned to bus service in 1938. Four of the Country Bus 5Q5s were transferred to Central Buses in 1938 and a further nine in 1942. The last fifty Qs were also by Park Royal but were long wheelbase thirty-two seat centre entrance Green Line coaches with full width drivers' cabs (Q 189–238; 6Q6).

In common with all Green Line coaches, the 6Q6s were converted to public ambulances at the outbreak of the Second World War and remained as such until being restored as coaches starting in October 1945. The public ambulances were equipped with eight or ten stretchers and supplied with a variety of medical items. The word 'AMBULANCE' was shown in large letters in the indicator box but otherwise no changes were made to their appearance.

As in the case of other large saloons, between December 1941 and June 1943 eighty-seven 4Q4s and forty 5Q5s had their seating re-arranged around the perimeter, to allow twenty standing passengers to be carried. This reduced their seating capacity to thirty-two and thirty-three respectively. One 6Q6 which did not return from ambulance duties was Q 217, which was severely damaged in July 1944 while at Elmers End when the garage was hit by a flying bomb. An attempt was made to repair the body but this proved to be impracticable and its remains were in store awaiting scrapping at the end of 1945. Q 1 was also in store, having been withdrawn from service on 30th September 1942. Otherwise all production Qs were still in use at the end of 1945.

The Central Bus 5Q5 version of the AEC 'Q' had its entrance ahead of the front wheels, a position made possible by the fact that no platform door was needed, thereby taking full advantage of the possibilities for increasing the capacity, which reached thirty-seven on this type. The roof of the Park Royal bodywork also had a slight slope but the use of a rear emergency door enabled the overall appearance of the body to be an improvement on the 4Q4. Note the minuscule blackout markings. W.J. Haynes

Q 226C standing by as a public ambulance at Chalk Farm in 1940 is already looking rather careworn. The Park Royal bodywork of the 6Q6s had a straight roof and behind the driver's cab was a neat and well proportioned design. The front end did not integrate well with the rest of the body and contained a spurious grille in the centre of the dash. D.W.K. Jones

The nearside of Q 226C taken at the end of the war when it had apparently been spruced up in the Lincoln green and white livery ready for its return to service, despite still being seconded to the Ministry of Health as an ambulance. The Q was not ideal as a coach as the position of the engine forced the use of longitudinal seats on the offside, in addition to those over the front wheels. R.H.G. Simpson

Chassis:	AEC 'Q' 762/0762
Engine:	AEC A167 6-cylinder 7.4 litre 95 bhp petrol (Q1);
	AEC A170 6-cylinder 7.7 litre 95 bhp oil (remainder)
Transmission:	AEC 4-speed crash (Q 1); AEC D133 4-speed direct selection preselective with fluid flywheel (remainder)
Bodywork:	LGOC (Chiswick) (Q 1); Birmingham Railway Carriage & Wagon Co. Ltd (Q 6–105, 186, 187); Park Royal (remainder).
Capacity:	B35C* (Q 1, 6–105, 186, 187); B37F* (106–185); DP32C (189–238);
L.T. code:	1Q1 (Q 1); 1/4 or 4Q4 or 4/1 (Q 6–105, 186, 187); 5Q5 (Q 106–185); 6Q6 (189–238)
Built:	1932 (Q 1); 1935/36 (4Q4); 1936 (5Q5); 1936/1937 (6Q6)
Number built:	233
Number in stock:	1.1.40: 233 31.12.45: 233
	* Buses converted to standee operation were B32+20C or B23+20F

Q		Q		Q	
1	GX5395	19	BXD541	33	BXD554
6	BXD527	20	BXD540	34	BXD555
7	BXD528	21	BXD542	35	BXD556
8	BXD529	22	BXD543	36	BXD557
9	BXD530	23	BXD544	37	BXD558
10	BXD531	24	BXD545	38	BXD559
11	BXD532	25	BXD546	39	BXD560
12	BXD533	26	BXD547	40	BXD561
13	BXD534	27	BXD548	41	BXD562
14	BXD535	28	BXD549	42	BXD563
15	BXD536	29	BXD550	43	BXD564
16	BXD537	30	BXD551	44	BXD565
17	BXD538	31	BXD552	45	BXD566
18	BXD539	32	BXD553	46	BXD567

Q

47	BXD568	111	CLE134	175	CLE198
48	BXD569	112	CLE135	176	CLE199
49	BXD570	113	CLE136	177	CLE200
50	BXD571	114	CLE137	178	CLE201
51	BXD572	115	CLE138	179	CLE202
52	BXD573	116	CLE139	180	CLE203
53	BXD574	117	CLE140	181	CLE204
54	BXD575	118	CLE141	182	CLE205
55	BXD576	119	CLE142	183	CLE206
56	CGJ161	120	CLE143	184	CLE207
57	CGJ162	121	CLE144	185	CLE208
58	CGJ163	122	CLE145	186	CLE127
59	CGJ164	123	CLE146	187	CLE128
60	CGJ165	124	CLE147	189	CXX382
61	CGJ166	125	CLE148	190	CXX383
62	CGJ167	126	CLE149	191	CXX384
63	CGJ168	127	CLE150	192	CXX385
64	CGJ169	128	CLE151	193	CXX386
65	CGJ170	129	CLE152	194	CXX387
66	CGJ171	130	CLE153	195	CXX388
67	CGJ172	131	CLE154	196	CXX389
68	CGJ173	132	CLE155	197	CXX390
69	CGJ174	133	CLE156	198	CXX391
70	CGJ175	134	CLE157	199	CXX392
71	CGJ176	135	CLE158	200	CXX393
72	CGJ177	136	CLE159	201	CXX394
73	CGJ178	137	CLE160	202	CXX395
74	CGJ179	138	CLE161	203	CXX396
75	CGJ180	139	CLE162	204	CXX397
76	CGJ181	140	CLE163	205	CXX398
77	CGJ182	141	CLE164	206	CXX399
78	CGJ183	142	CLE165	207	CXX400
79	CGJ184	143	CLE166	208	CXX401
80	CGJ185	144	CLE167	209	CXX402
81	CGJ186	145	CLE168	210	CXX403
82	CGJ187	146	CLE169	211	CXX404
83	CGJ188	147	CLE170	212	CXX405
84	CGJ189	148	CLE171	213	CXX406
85	CGJ190	149	CLE172	214	DGX220
86	CGJ191	150	CLE173	215	DGX221
87	CGJ192	151	CLE174	216	DGX222
88	CGJ193	152	CLE175	217	DGX223
89	CGJ195	153	CLE176	218	DGX224
90	CGJ194	154	CLE177	219	DGX225
91	CGJ196	155	CLE178	220	DGX226
92	CGJ197	156	CLE179	221	DGX227
93	CGJ198	157	CLE180	222	DGX228
94	CGJ199	158	CLE181	223	DGX229
95	CGJ200	159	CLE182	224	DGX230
96	CGJ201	160	CLE183	225	DGX231
97	CGJ202	161	CLE184	226	DGX232
98	CGJ203	162	CLE185	227	DGX233
99	CGJ204	163	CLE186	228	DGX234
100	CGJ205	164	CLE187	229	DGX235
101	CGJ206	165	CLE188	230	DGX236
102	CGJ207	166	CLE189	231	DGX237
103	CGJ208	167	CLE190	232	DGX238
104	CGJ209	168	CLE191	233	DGX239
105	CGJ210	169	CLE192	234	DGX240
106	CLE129	170	CLE193	235	DGX241
107	CLE130	171	CLE194	236	DGX242
108	CLE131	172	CLE195	237	DGX243
109	CLE132	173	CLE196	238	DGX244
110	CLE133	174	CLE197		

The role of the twenty-seater diminished markedly during the war and Weymann bodied C10B was one of the casualties, being withdrawn in January 1943 and sold to the Belgian Economic Commission in 1945. C.F. Klapper

C

The Leyland Cub was chosen by London Transport in 1935 as its standard one-man bus and was used to replace the many different types of small bus inherited from Independent operators. Ninety-eight buses were eventually owned, including the prototype C 1 and one acquired from Charles Russett and Sons of St Albans (C 76, withdrawn in 1938). Of the remainder, the first seventy-four were Country Area buses bodied by Short Bros. of Rochester (C 2–75; 2C2) built in 1935 and twenty-two were Central Area buses, bodied by Weymann in 1936 (C77–98; 1/2C2). There were also eight Park Royal bodied forward-control 1½-deckers built in 1936 for the Inter-Station service (C106–113; 3C3). The intervening numbers (99–105, plus 114) were allocated to eight Leyland Cub lorries (numbered C99L etc. in the Service Vehicle fleet).

The C class did not suffer any losses from enemy action during the war but the number needed for service was cut substantially as the big increases in demand for bus services in the Country Area and the drive towards economy of operation led to the use of bigger buses wherever possible. The number of twenty-seaters scheduled for service fell from exactly one hundred at the outbreak of war to only forty-one at the end of 1945, the greatest drop being in the Central Area where only seven were required in 1945. Much of the decline was absorbed by the withdrawal of the DA class but thirty-one bus Cubs were withdrawn from service during these years. The Inter-Station service was withdrawn in the autumn of 1939 and there was no immediate use for the vehicles but in December 1942 and January 1943 they were painted khaki and put on loan to the Entertainments National Service Association (ENSA) to provide transport around Britain for the troupes of entertainers. Four (C 106, 109, 111, 112) were returned in August 1943 in readiness for the restoration of a limited Inter-Station service, shared with one ST, in December 1943. During 1944 and 1945, the Cubs on the Inter-Station service were replaced progressively by specially modified STs and none was in service at the end of 1945, the other four still being with ENSA. In the aftermath of the war, in November 1945, thirty of the stored bus Cubs went to the Belgian Economic Mission for relief work in continental Europe, the exception being C 1 which remained in stock at the end of the year.

Chassis:	Leyland Cub KP3 (C 1); KPO3 (C 2–75, 77–98); SKPZ2 (C 106–113)		
Engine:	Leyland 6-cylinder side-valve 4.4 litre 55 bhp petrol (C 1); Leyland 6-cylinder 4.4 litre direct injection 55 bhp oil (C 2–50, 52–75); Leyland 4.7 litre indirect injection 65 bhp (C 77–98); Leyland 4.7 litre 65 bhp ohv petrol (C 106–113)		
Transmission:	Leyland 4-speed crash		
Bodywork:	LPTB (Chiswick) (C 1); Short Bros (C 2–74); Weymann (C 77–98); Park Royal (C 106–113)		
Capacity:	B20F (C 1–98); DP20F (C106–113)		
L.T. codes:	1C1 (C 1); 2C2 (C 2–75); 1/2C2 (C 77–98); 3C3 (C 106–113)		
Built:	1934 (C 1); 1935 (2–75); 1936 (C 77–98, 106–113)		
Number built:	106		
Number in stock:	1.1.45: 105; 31.12.45: 75		

C		Date out of stock	C		Date out of stock	C		Date out of stock
1	AYV717		36	BXD661		71	BXD696	27.11.45
2	BXD631		37	BXD662		72	BXD697	27.11.45
3	BXD627		38	BXD663		73	BXD698	
4	BXD628		39	BXD664		74	BXD699	
5	BXD629	26.11.45	40	BXD665		75	BXD700	27.11.45
6	BXD632	27.11.45	41	BXD666		77	CLE105	
7	BXD630		42	BXD667		78	CLE106	
8	BXD633		43	BXD668	26.11.45	79	CLE107	27.11.45
9	BXD634	27.11.45	44	BXD669		80	CLE108	27.11.45
10	BXD635	26.11.45	45	BXD670		81	CLE109	
11	BXD636		46	BXD671	27.11.45	82	CLE110	
12	BXD637	26.11.45	47	BXD672		83	CLE111	26.11.45
13	BXD638		48	BXD673	26.11.45	84	CLE112	27.11.45
14	BXD639		49	BXD674		85	CLE113	26.11.45
15	BXD640		50	BXD675		86	CLE114	26.11.45
16	BXD641		51	BXD676	27.11.45	87	CLE115	27.11.45
17	BXD642		52	BXD677		88	CLE116	
18	BXD643		53	BXD678		89	CLE117	27.11.45
19	BXD644		54	BXD679	26.11.45	90	CLE118	
20	BXD645		55	BXD680	26.11.45	91	CLE119	
21	BXD646		56	BXD681		92	CLE120	
22	BXD647		57	BXD682		93	CLE121	
23	BXD648		58	BXD683		94	CLE122	
24	BXD649		59	BXD684		95	CLE123	
25	BXD650		60	BXD685		96	CLE124	27.11.45
26	BXD651		61	BXD686		97	CLE125	
27	BXD652	27.11.45	62	BXD687	27.11.45	98	CLE126	
28	BXD653		63	BXD688		106	CLX543	
29	BXD654	26.11.45	64	BXD689		107	CLX544	
30	BXD655		65	BXD690		108	CLX545	
31	BXD656		66	BXD691		109	CLX546	
32	BXD657		67	BXD692	27.11.45	110	CLX547	
33	BXD658	26.11.45	68	BXD693	27.11.45	111	CLX548	
34	BXD659		69	BXD694		112	CLX549	
35	BXD660	26.11.45	70	BXD695		113	CLX550	

C 99–105/114 were service vehicles

The underfloor-engined TF may well have marked the beginning of a new phase in single-deck design but for the interruption of the war, which started only six months after the first production vehicles, including Chiswick-bodied TF 18, went into service. The full potential for increasing capacity above the mere thirty-four actually obtained, the same as a 10T10/1, was vitiated by the need to have a sliding door, which governed the position of the entrance. The area over the nearside front wheel was wasted, the space being occupied by a radiator filler cap. D.W.K. Jones

TF

The prototype TF 1, which was taken into stock on 10th July 1937, was a revolutionary new design by Leyland Motors, incorporating an underfloor engine for the first time and including air operated brakes and gearbox. The Leyland body was similar in many respects to the contemporary Chiswick designs but with swept down front and rear saloon windows, streamlined mudguards and an unusual driver's cab with its windscreen rising high into the front dome to accommodate a high driving position. To allow the inclusion of a sliding door, the entrance was behind the front axle and the area ahead of the nearside bulkhead was effectually a wide wing. There were two production batches: twelve Private Hire coaches (TF 2–13) with Park Royal 33-seat bodywork; and seventy-five Green Line coaches with LPTB (Chiswick) 34-seat bodywork (TF 14–88). The basic layout was the same as on TF 1 but significant changes included a more conventional driving position and cab, a straight window line and the incorporation of a radiator and filler cap in the nearside wing. TF 1 was rebuilt with the same type of cab and radiator in 1940. The Private Hire coaches also differed in having glass cant panels for sightseeing, a sliding roof, radio, an offside emergency exit and no rear destination indicator.

The production TFs were delivered during 1939 but saw little service as the Green Line coaches were withdrawn for use as public ambulances on the outbreak of war and based in small numbers at various Central Bus garages. Eleven were restored as coaches in December 1945 but the remainder were still fitted out as ambulances at the end of the year. The Private Hire coaches were used by Country Buses for a time, with their cant panels painted over as a blackout precaution, but were delicensed in November 1939. TF 1 and TF 9 were relicensed in October 1940 for limited private hire work but the remaining eleven Private Hire coaches remained in store and were destroyed when the former Tilling premises at Bull Yard Peckham were bombed on 22nd October 1940.

The nearside of TF 69C, a 2TF2, showing the partly opened sliding door, the area in front of which was occupied by a double seat. **The high floor line required to accommodate the underfloor engine enabled a straight waistline to be used, giving the body a slightly tidier look than the contemporary 10T10.** R.H.G. Simpson

Chassis:	Leyland Tiger FEC
Engine:	Leyland 8.6 litre direct injection 94 bhp oil, horizontal.
Transmission:	AEC D132 air-operated direct selection preselective with fluid flywheel.
Bodywork:	Leyland (TF 1); Park Royal (TF 2–13); LPTB (Chiswick) (TF 14–88)
Capacity:	DP34F (TF 1, 14–88); C33F (TF 2–13)
L.T. code:	1TF1 (TF 1); 2TF2 (TF 14–88); 2TF3 (TF 2–13)
Built:	1937 (TF 1); 1939 (TF 2–88)
Number built:	88
Number in stock:	1.1.40: 88 31.12.45: 77

TF		Date out of stock	TF		Date out of stock	TF		Date out of stock
1	DYL904		31	FJJ642		61	FJJ672	
2	FJJ603	22.10.40 b	32	FJJ643		62	FJJ673	
3	FJJ604	22.10.40 b	33	FJJ644		63	FJJ674	
4	FJJ605	22.10.40 b	34	FJJ645		64	FJJ761	
5	FJJ606	22.10.40 b	35	FJJ646		65	FJJ762	
6	FJJ607	22.10.40 b	36	FJJ647		66	FJJ763	
7	FJJ608	22.10.40 b	37	FJJ648		67	FJJ764	
8	FJJ609	22.10.40 b	38	FJJ649		68	FJJ765	
9	FJJ610		39	FJJ650		69	FJJ766	
10	FJJ611	22.10.40 b	40	FJJ651		70	FJJ767	
11	FJJ612	22.10.40 b	41	FJJ652		71	FJJ768	
12	FJJ613	22.10.40 b	42	FJJ653		72	FJJ769	
13	FJJ614	22.10.40 b	43	FJJ654		73	FJJ770	
14	FJJ615		44	FJJ655		74	FJJ771	
15	FJJ616		45	FJJ656		75	FJJ772	
16	FJJ617		46	FJJ657		76	FJJ773	
17	FJJ618		47	FJJ658		77	FJJ774	
18	FJJ629		48	FJJ659		78	FJJ775	
19	FJJ630		49	FJJ660		79	FJJ776	
20	FJJ631		50	FJJ661		80	FJJ777	
21	FJJ632		51	FJJ662		81	FXT41	
22	FJJ633		52	FJJ663		82	FXT42	
23	FJJ634		53	FJJ664		83	FXT43	
24	FJJ635		54	FJJ665		84	FXT44	
25	FJJ636		55	FJJ666		85	FXT45	
26	FJJ637		56	FJJ667		86	FXT46	
27	FJJ638		57	FJJ668		87	FXT47	
28	FJJ639		58	FJJ669		88	FXT48	
29	FJJ640		59	FJJ670				
30	FJJ641		60	FJJ671				

b Destroyed by bombing

The CRs were the first rear-engined buses to be put into service in Britain but the beginning of a world war was not the best time for such a revolutionary design to arrive. The CRs paid for this by being withdrawn within less than three years, often replaced by larger buses. The neat design, which was very similar to the equally revolutionary TF class, incorporated an emergency door in the second bay on the offside and an unusual design of rear hub with a large projecting disc. Malcolm Papes collection

CR

The CR was a revolutionary new version of the Cub chassis designed by Leyland in conjunction with London Transport in 1937 when prototype CR 1B was built. The standard Leyland 4.4 litre engine was placed transversely at the rear of the chassis, along with the gearbox and radiator. The bodywork, built by the LPTB at Chiswick Works, was based on the Board's contemporary design standards. A half-cab layout was adopted, with the passenger doorway immediately behind the front wheels, the area above the nearside wheel not being used. A production batch of forty-eight to basically the same design but with the 4.7 litre indirect injection engine, was ordered to replace the remaining DA and BD class vehicles.

The first four entered service at Kingston garage in September 1939. Six (CR 12B–17B) were painted green for Country Bus service and were allocated to Windsor garage. Thirty-five had been licensed by the end of the year and this remained the maximum at any one time, although forty-two had seen service by February 1941. Wartime service cuts and the increasing use of larger buses had reduced the number of twenty-seaters required for service and this trend continued throughout the war years. Coincidentally the revolutionary rear-engined design was suffering many problems which were putting a severe strain on the scarce engineering resources and the CRs were therefore progressively delicensed and put into store as older Cubs became available to replace them. The green ones were withdrawn in November 1940 and May 1941 but the first red CR was taken out of service as early as July 1940. However, the major withdrawals in the Central Area took place in May, June and July 1942, after which all the survivors were in store, where they still were at the end of 1945. At this time CRs 36, 38, 40, 41, 42, 44 and 45 had not yet been licensed.

An early loss from the class was CR 18 which was one of the buses at Bull Yard, Peckham when it was bombed in October 1940.

The engine of the CR, discreetly contained within the body area, was mounted vertically and transversely and there were hinged panels on each side to give excellent access for maintenance. In keeping with Chiswick's high design standards, the rear window and the rail across the engine compartment inside the saloon, curved in harmony with the shape of the roof and some restrained embellishment was applied to the grille. The rear white blackout disc can be seen peeping out from behind the grille of CR 2. John Gillham

Chassis:	Leyland REC
Engine:	Leyland 6-cylinder 4.4 litre direct injection 55 bhp oil mounted transversely (CR 1);
	Leyland 4.7 litre indirect injection 65 bhp oil (CR 2–49)
Transmission:	Leyland 4-speed crash (helical third gear)
Bodywork:	LPTB
Capacity:	B20F
L.T. code:	1CR1 (CR 1); 2CR2 (CR 2–49)
Built:	1939
Number built:	49
Number in stock:	1.1.40: 46 31.12.45: 48

CR		Date out of stock	CR		Date into stock
CR		*Date out of stock*	**CR**		*Date into stock*
1	ELP294		18	FXT124	22.10.40 b
2	FXT108		19	FXT125	
3	FXT109		20	FXT126	
4	FXT110		21	FXT127	
5	FXT111		22	FXT128	
6	FXT112		23	FXT129	
7	FXT113		24	FXT130	
8	FXT114		25	FXT131	
9	FXT115		26	FXT132	
10	FXT116		27	FXT133	
11	FXT117		28	FXT134	
12	FXT118		29	FXT135	
13	FXT119		30	FXT136	
14	FXT120		31	FXT137	
15	FXT121		32	FXT138	
16	FXT122		33	FXT139	
17	FXT123		34	FXT140	
35	FXT141				
36	FXT142				
37	FXT143				
38	FXT144				
39	FXT145				
40	FXT146				
41	FXT147				
42	FXT148				
43	FXT149				
44	FXT150				
45	FXT151				
46	FXT152				
47	FXT153	13.2.40			
48	FXT154	11.1.40			
49	FXT155	29.1.40			

b Destroyed by bombing

The LTC private hire coaches were also in use as ambulances throughout the war and LTC 1, which was among the many allocated to Chalk Farm, was still looking reasonably smart in its two-tone green livery at the end of the period. The thirty-seat Weymann bodies were similar in general design to the 9T9s but were shorter because the wheelbase of these six-wheelers was less than that of the Regals. R.H.G. Simpson

LTC

The LTC class was purchased in 1937 to replace the life expired fleet of Private Hire coaches, mainly T class AEC Regals. The AEC Renown chassis was chosen in order to reduce wheel arch intrusion in the saloon and petrol engines were specified for quiet running. They differed from the LT class Renowns in having fully floating rear axles. Their Weymann 30-seat bodywork was similar to the 9T9 but without a rear destination indicator, built-up bonnet and wing assembly or bumper bar. They were fitted with sliding roof, radio and individual coach seats arranged in staggered pairs.

On the outbreak of war in September 1939, the LTCs were converted to public ambulances and remained as such until December 1945.

Chassis:	AEC Renown 663
Engine:	AEC A145 7.4 litre 110 bhp petrol
Transmission:	AEC D132 4-speed direct acting preselective with fluid flywheel.
Bodywork:	Weymann
Capacity:	C30F
L.T. code:	1LTC1
Built:	1937/1938
Number built:	24
Number in stock:	1.1.40: 24 31.12.45: 24

LTC

1	EGO505	9	EGO513	17	EGO521
2	EGO506	10	EGO514	18	EGO522
3	EGO507	11	EGO515	19	EGO523
4	EGO508	12	EGO516	20	EGO524
5	EGO509	13	EGO517	21	EGO525
6	EGO510	14	EGO518	22	EGO526
7	EGO511	15	EGO519	23	EGO527
8	EGO512	16	EGO520	24	EGO528